Name

Class

Teacher

Safar Islamic Studies Textbook 3

Part of the Safar Learn about Islam Series

Sixth edition, 2019 (Reprinted, 2021)

First published 2013

Published by

Safar Publications, London, England

www.safarpublications.org

info@safarpublications.org

Edited by

Hasan Ali

Muhammed Ahmed

Designed and illustrated by

Reedwan Iqbal

ISBN 978-1-912437-28-3

A catalogue record for this book is available from the British Library.

Printed in Turkey

Safar Islamic Studies Textbook 3

Safar Publications

Edited by

Hasan Ali

Muhammed Ahmed

Designed and illustrated by

Reedwan Iqbal

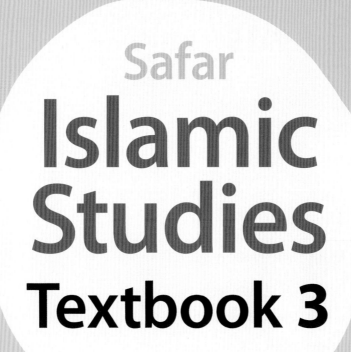

Contents

🏃 Practical lesson; W Week number

Term 3

Aqīdah, *Fiqh*, History, *Sīrah*, Personal development

Transliteration key

إ أ ء	ʾ	A light catch in the breath; Qurʾān, *ʿIshāʾ*
ا	a ā	*Allāhu akbar*, Islām
ب	b	*Bismillāh*
ت	t	*Takbīr*
ث	th	Pronounced as the *th* in thin or thirst; *thawāb*
ج	j	Jannah
ح	ḥ	Tensely breathed *h* sound, produced by a strong expulsion of air from the chest and by narrowing the passage in the depth of the throat; *Ḥaj*
خ	kh	Guttural *ch* as in the Scottish loch with the mouth hollowed to produce a full sound; *ākhirah*
د	d	Pronounced lightly; *duʿāʾ*
ذ	dh	Should be pronounced as the *th* in this or that; *Adhān*

ر	r	*Raḥmah*
ز	z	*Zakāh*
س	s	*Sūrah*
ش	sh	*Shahādah*
ص	ṣ	A heavy *s* pronounced with the mouth hollowed to produce a full sound; *Ṣalāh*
ض	ḍ	A heavy *d/dh* pronounced with the mouth hollowed to produce a full sound; Ramaḍān
ط	ṭ	A heavy *t* pronounce with the mouth hollowed to produce a full sound; *shayṭān*
ظ	ẓ	A heavy *dh* pronounced with the mouth hollowed to produce a full sound; *Ẓuhr*
ع	ʿ ʿa ʿi ʿu	Pronounced from the throat, by narrowing the passage in the depth of the throat; *ʿAṣr, ʿIshāʾ, ʿUmrah*
غ	gh	Pronounced with the mouth hollowed to produce a full sound; *ghusl*

ف	f	*Fajr*
ق	q	A guttural *q* sound with the mouth hollowed to produce a full sound; Qur'ān
ك	k	*Kalām*
ل	l	*Labbayk*
م	m	*Mu'min*
ن	n	*Nūr*
و	w ū	*Tawḥīd, wuḍū'*
ه	h	*Hijrah*
ي	y ī	Ubayy, *īman*, Quraysh

Honorifics

Subḥānahū wa ta'ālā follows the mention of Allāh. It means, "May He be glorified and exalted."

Sallallāhu 'alayhi wa sallam follows the mention of Prophet Muḥammad. It means, "May Allāh bless him and give him peace."

'Alayhis salām follows the mention of a prophet

or a messenger. It is translated as, "May the peace of Allāh be upon him."

عليهم السلام *'Alayhimus salām* follows the mention of more than one prophet or messenger.

رضي الله عنه *Raḍiyallāhu 'anhu* follows the mention of a male Companion of the Prophet. It means, "May Allāh be pleased with him."

رضي الله عنها *Raḍiyallāhu 'anhā* follows the mention of a female Companion. It means, "May Allāh be pleased with her."

رضي الله عنهم *Raḍiyallāhu 'anhum* follows the mention of more than one Companion It means, "May Allāh be pleased with them."

رحمه الله تعالى *Raḥimahullāh ta'ālā* is follows the mention of a pious person. It means, "May Allāh, the Exalted, have mercy on him."

Honorific titles and forms of address, such as *Sayyidunā, Ummul mu'minīn, Amīrul mu'minīn*, have been omitted in the text. The readers and teachers are encouraged to use these at all occurences.

Preface

In 1998, our first year, we purchased a number of Islamic Studies curricula from across the globe. However, every curriculum came with its own weaknesses – some more than others – but temporarily, we used various parts of different curricula to continue teaching.

For the long-term, we decided to create a comprehensive cross-curriculum, which would be enjoyable for children and make a positive impression on their identity and moral character, as well as imbuing them with the spirit of traditional Islam while allowing them to live in harmony with the modern world.

By 2002, I had drafted a 50-page syllabus which outlined much of what should be taught. However, the challenge then, was to organise it in an age-appropriate manner and to create a progressive system of learning. For the next few years, various staff members voluntarily created individual lessons and trialled them; their feedback helped us immensely to re-shape the syllabus model.

In 2007, I led a team to further this work, namely, Amjad Shaikh, Mohibur Rahman, Shamim Sobur, A. Mushahid Kadir, Sofwan Ahmed and Shahid Bukhari. By 2010, we published the first edition: an in-depth yet concise curriculum, which had all core subjects in year-based textbooks. These books also addressed contemporary issues through weekly lessons, covered over a full academic year by building on core knowledge from previous books. A second full colour edition was published in 2013, which was a substantial improvement on the first edition.

Much has improved in the current edition of the series. The language and content have been further refined, ensuring a higher degree of concision.

Each textbook comes with schemes of work and also has a workbook with two tiers of assessment, based on Bloom's Taxonomy of learning objectives. The most unique aspect of this Islamic Studies series is that it is part of a curriculum composed of four interlinking parts. The other three parts being Tajwīd, Memorisation and Arabic.

Finally, we thank Allāh سبحانه وتعالى for giving us this opportunity to serve His *dīn* and pray that He makes the work a true success in both worlds for all those who use it. We ask the reader to pray for us and all those who have contributed to this work, both academically and financially.

Your brother in Islam,
Hasan Ali, MA Education (Psychology)
29 April 2014, 28 Jumādal Ākhirah 1435

Note to parents

As a parent, you can play a key role in improving your child's academic attainment as well as forming good manners. Good quality home learning contributes more to a child's intellectual and social development than formal class-based activities. Regularly talking to your child about their learning and helping them through the process, will greatly increase the benefit gained from this series.

It is important that you allocate some time during the week to revise what has been previously covered with your child in class. The amount of time needed for this will vary according to the ability of your child as well as the complexity of the material. This activity is essential in helping you understand your child's progress and development, as well as supporting the child to revise and retain key learning points.

Reading to your child

Reading together not only helps instil confidence in a child but also creates a positive attitude towards learning. Children who read with their families on a regular basis, develop a love of reading that lasts a lifetime. This activity is integral to our teaching methodology.

As parents, you should try your best to:

- Read to your child as often as possible.
- Listen to your child read aloud.
- Ask your child to explain what they have read (or you have read to them) in order to check comprehension. This is an effective method to help strengthen your child's understanding.
- Talk to your child about what has been read. Talking will help your child develop critical thinking skills.
- Set expectations for your child and be clear in articulating these to them.

In class, teachers will not read the stories in the book word for word but rather, deliver the story in a dramatised narrative. This leaves you with a good opportunity to read the story together with your child. and discuss the morals and lessons contained within the stories.

Workbook and resources

A workbook is available for each textbook in order to aid your child's learning; please refer to the workbook for further guidance. Resources are also available on our website.

Practical checklist

Parents are role models for their children. When children see their parents getting involved in their learning, they tend to be much more enthusiastic about engaging with the content.

Some of the lessons in this textbook have practical aspects which parents can help the child practice at home. Other lessons are best taught by embodying the teachings yourself and being a role model for the child. Below, are lists of such lessons contained in this book as well as a recap of previous lessons.

Lessons: previous

- Deeds: aim to maintain a higher level of consciousness of the consequences of actions, positive or negative. Encourage your child to do good deeds by reminding them that Allāh سبحانه وتعالى will reward them with Jannah.
- Cleanliness: ensure your child knows how to clean himself properly.
- Good Manners and friendship: discuss the importance of having good manners as well as teaching them manners and good etiquettes to use in their day-to-day lives. Also, discuss the importance of keeping good friends and good company.

Lessons: current

- Jannah and Jahannam: aim to maintain a higher level of consciousness of the consequences of all actions. Encourage your child to do good deeds by reminding them that Allāh سبحانه وتعالى will reward them.
- *Ṣalāh*: the textbook contains a practical lesson on *Ṣalāh*.

You should discuss the importance of *Ṣalāh* and help your child learn the core actions of performing *Ṣalāh* correctly.

- *Wuḍū'*: observe your child performing *wuḍū'*, ensuring that they perform it properly while reading the relevant supplications loudly, as detailed in the textbook.
- *Ghusl*: ensure your child performs *ghusl* regularly, especially on Fridays.
- Respecting people and good manners: discuss the importance of respecting all members of the community.
- Manners of eating and drinking and *ḥalāl* food: practice the manners at home. Also, discuss the importance of eating *ḥalāl* food.
- Manners of the *masjid*: teach your child the manners of visiting the *masjid*. Also, try your best to take your child to visit the *masjid* regularly.
- TV, music, games and the internet: it is important to ensure there is moderation and adequate monitoring of the types of content children are exposed to. Also, discuss the harms of music.

Essential Revision

Core revision

The five pillars of Islām

1. *Shahādah*
2. *Ṣalāh*
3. *Ṣawm* (fasting)
4. *Zakāh*
5. *Ḥajj*

The six articles of faith

1. I believe in Allāh.
2. I believe in angels.
3. I believe in His books.
4. I believe in His messengers.
5. I believe in the Last Day.
6. I believe in destiny (*qadar).*

Wuḍū'

Wuḍū' means to wash some parts of the body with water to perform *Ṣalāh* or touch the Qur'ān. The actions of *wuḍū'* are:

1. Making intention and saying *Bismillāh*
2. Washing the hands

3. Rinsing the mouth
4. Rinsing the nose
5. Washing the face
6. Washing the arms
7. Wiping the head, ears and back of neck
8. Washing the feet

Breakers of *wuḍū'*

- Sleeping
- Using the toilet
- Passing wind
- Bleeding
- Laughing in *Ṣalāh*
- Vomiting

Ghusl

Ghusl means to clean the entire body by taking a bath/shower. It is *sunnah* to bathe every Friday. Actions of *ghusl* are:

1. Washing the hands
2. Performing *wuḍū'*
3. Washing the mouth by gargling
4. Rinsing the nose
5. Pouring water over the entire body

Times of *Ṣalāh*

- *Fajr*: before sunrise
- *Ẓuhr*: early afternoon
- *ʿAṣr*: late afternoon
- *Maghrib*: after sunset
- *ʿIshāʾ*: night time

Actions of *Ṣalāh*

- *Takbīr*: to raise your hands at the beginning of *Ṣalāh* and say, *"Allāhu akbar"*
- *Qiyām*: to stand during the prayer
- *Rukūʿ*: to bow down
- *Sajdah*: to prostrate
- *Salām*: to turn your head at the end of *Ṣalāh*, once to the right and once to the left

Zakāh and *Ṣadaqah*

- *Zakāh:* this is a pillar of Islām and it means that a rich Muslim must give a small amount of money to poor people once a year.
- *Ṣadaqah* also means to give money to the poor (charity). This charity is given by any Muslim at any time. *Ṣadaqah* does not have to be money. It can be actions, such as smiling or doing something to make someone happy.

Further revision

Names of Allāh

- Al-Raḥmān – the Most Merciful
- Al-Raḥīm – the Most Kind
- Al-ʿAlīm – the All-Knowing
- Al-Baṣīr – the All-Seeing
- Al-Samīʿ – the All-Hearing

Angels

The four main angels are:

- Jibrīl عليه السلام: he brought messages to the prophets.
- Mīkā'īl عليه السلام: he controls the rain and food.
- Malakul Mawt عليه السلام: he is the angel of death.
- Isrāfīl عليه السلام: he will blow the trumpet on the Last Day.

Allah's messengers and prophets

Allāh سبحانه وتعالى sent many prophets and messengers to this world. Prophets and messengers teach people about Allāh سبحانه وتعالى and how to be good.

- Muslims believe in all the messengers and prophets, such as Ādam, Nuḥ, Mūsā and ʿĪsā عليهم السلام.
- The Last Prophet was Muḥammad صلى الله عليه وسلم. There will be no other prophets or messengers sent to this world.

Allāh's books

The four main books are:

- The Tawrāh revealed to Mūsā عليه السلام.
- The Zabūr revealed to Dāwūd عليه السلام.
- The Injīl revealed to ʿĪsā عليه السلام.
- The Qurʾān revealed to Prophet Muḥammad صلى الله عليه وسلم. This is the last book sent by Allāh سبحانه وتعالى to all humans.

Deeds

- We have been sent in this world to do good actions. Good deeds lead to Paradise. Bad deeds may lead to punishment. We can get rid of our bad deeds by seeking Allāh's سبحانه وتعالى forgiveness and doing more good deeds. Also, we need to say sorry to all people we hurt or harm.

Salām

When we meet a Muslim, we say, "*Assalāmu ʿalaykum.*" When we respond, we say, "*Wa ʿalaykumus salām.*"

Bismillāh

We mention the name of Allāh سبحانه وتعالى before we start doing anything. When we say, "*Bismillāh,*" Allāh سبحانه وتعالى gives us blessings and makes things easy for us.

Cleanliness *(ṭahārah)*

- The Prophet said, "Keeping clean is half of faith."
- Keeping clean is very important in Islām.

Using the toilet

- I go into the toilet with my left foot first and say the *duʿāʾ*.
- I go into the toilet without my socks and use the slippers that are meant to be used in the toilet.
- I should sit down to use the toilet and take care not to make my clothes unclean.
- I should not talk in the toilet (unless I need help) and I must not say any *duʿāʾ*.
- When I have finished, I use water and tissue to clean myself.
- Finally, I flush the toilet, wash my hands and leave the toilet with my right foot first and say the *duʿāʾ*.

Names of Allāh

Al-Qādir

Al-Qādir means the All-Powerful. Allāh سبحانه وتعالى can do whatever He wants and nobody can stop Him. Allāh سبحانه وتعالى has power over His creation but they do not have power over Him. Allāh سبحانه وتعالى sometimes shows His power so that we do not forget that He is All-Powerful.

An example is when Muslims went to Egypt, during the time of ʿUmar رضي الله عنه. ʿUmar رضي الله عنه sent one of the Prophet's صلى الله عليه وسلم Companions, ʿAmr رضي الله عنه, to become the new leader of Egypt. Every year, the water of the River Nile would become very shallow. It was the belief of the Egyptian people that if they sacrificed a beautiful young girl by throwing her into the river, it would fill up with water again. This was very strange and worrying for the Muslims and the new leader ʿAmr رضي الله عنه.

So ʿAmr رضي الله عنه wrote a letter to ʿUmar رضي الله عنه explaining the situation. When ʿUmar رضي الله عنه received ʿAmr's رضي الله عنه letter, he turned to Allāh سبحانه وتعالى. He knew only Allāh سبحانه وتعالى could make the river flow again. He then sent a letter back to ʿAmr رضي الله عنه to give to the River Nile.

The letter said, "O River! If you flow according to your own wish then we do not need you but if you flow according to the will of Allāh, then we ask you to rise and not become shallow again." All the people gathered to see what would happen to the River Nile. To their amazement, it started flowing again.[1] This is how Allāh سبحانه وتعالى showed His power to the people. The River Nile has never became shallow again after that.

Aṣ-Ṣamad

Allāh سبحانه وتعالى is independent. He does not need anyone. Everyone is in need of Him. We need air to breathe, water to drink and food to eat. Just like us, other creations in the universe also rely on different things. Allāh سبحانه وتعالى does not rely on anything at all. The Prophet صلى الله عليه وسلم said that Allāh سبحانه وتعالى says, "O My servants! If the first of you and the last of you, the humans among you and the jinn among you were to stand in one place and each of you were to wish whatever he wanted, I will be able to grant you all your wishes in one go but nothing would decrease in My kingdom, not even the amount of a tiny droplet of water at the end of a needle if it were dipped in the ocean."[2]

Al-Khāliq

Allāh سبحانه وتعالى is the Creator. He created us and the whole universe. He made everything the way it is. Allāh سبحانه وتعالى created angels from light, jinns from fire and humans from clay. He made our bodies, gave us skin colour and made us special. He created the mountains, the seas, the trees, the sun and the moon. In fact, He created everything. There is no other creator besides Allāh سبحانه وتعالى.

Al-Bidāyah wan-Nihāyah; [2,3] Muslim, [4] Bukhārī

Ar-Razzāq

Allāh سبحانه وتعالى is the provider. He gives us all the things we need. Allāh سبحانه وتعالى sends down rain which helps the plants grow. The plants become food for us and for animals too. Without Allāh سبحانه وتعالى, we would not have any food to eat or clothes to wear. The Prophet صلى الله عليه وسلم said, "Allāh سبحانه وتعالى says, 'O My servants! All of you are hungry except for those whom I have fed, so ask Me to give you food and I shall feed you. O My servants! All of you are naked except those whom I have clothed, so ask Me for clothes and I shall clothe you.'"[3]

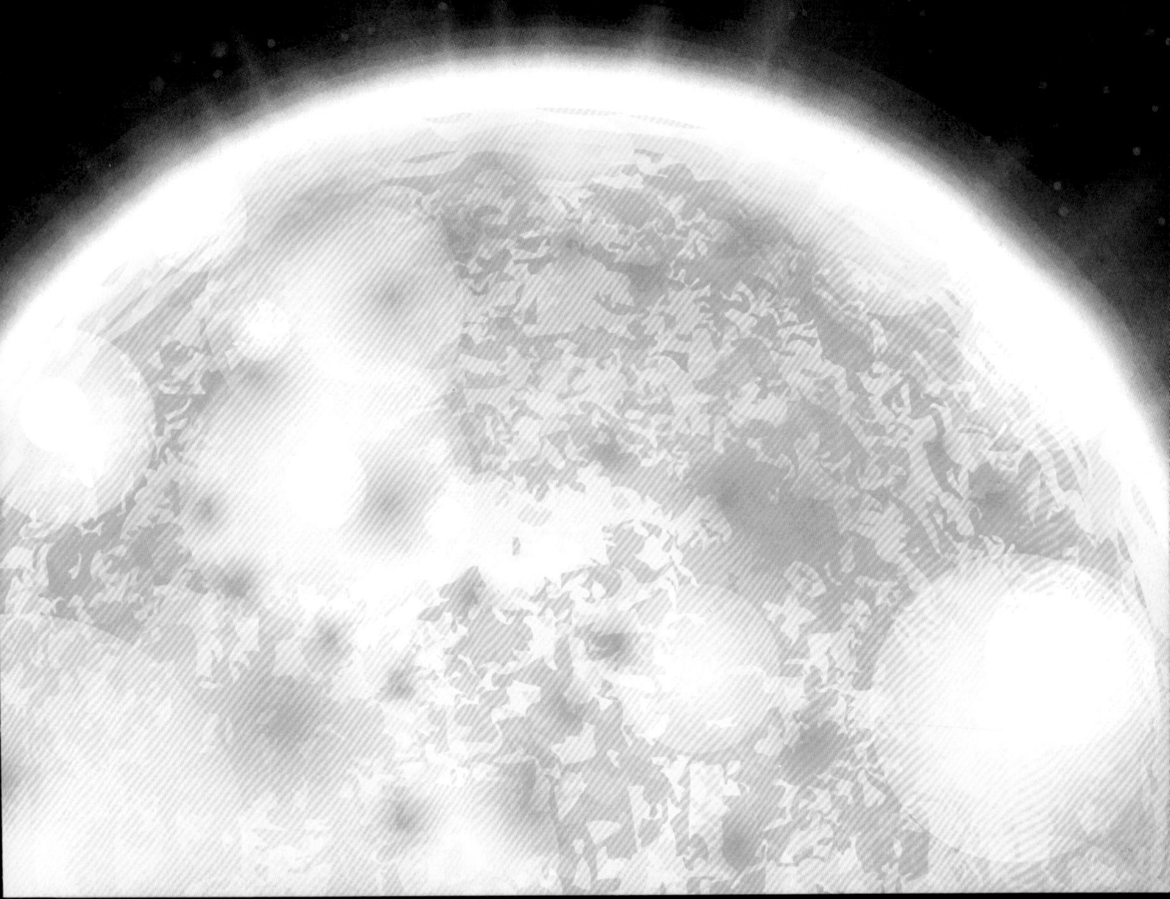

Al-Mujib

Allāh سبحانه وتعالى answers our *du'ā's*. He loves those who ask from Him. He helps us when we are in trouble and He makes things easy for us. When we are ill, He is the One who cures us. When we are hungry He is the One who feeds us.

Our Prophet صلى الله عليه وسلم said, "Three people were once on a journey and they faced a storm. The three of them went into a cave to take shelter. Suddenly, a rock fell from the mountain and blocked the entrance of the cave. There was no way to get out. So they all turned to Allāh and made *du'ā'* to Him. Each one of them remembered something they did for the sake of Allāh سبحانه وتعالى and said to Him, 'O Allāh if I really did this for Your sake then remove this rock from the entrance'. After the first person's *du'ā'*, Allāh سبحانه وتعالى moved the rock slightly but it was not enough for them to come out. The same happened with the second person's *du'ā'*, but on the third person's *du'ā'* Allāh سبحانه وتعالى moved it enough for them to come out."[4]

Hābīl and Qābīl

Prophet Ādam عليه السلام had two sons, Hābīl and Qābīl. As a father and a prophet, Ādam عليه السلام would tell his sons to do many good things. One day he advised his sons to make a sacrifice for Allāh سبحانه وتعالى, in order to thank Him for all the blessings they had. He explained to them that they should give the best of their wealth, for Allāh سبحانه وتعالى is pure and only accepts that which is pure.

Both Hābīl and Qābīl put forward their sacrifices to Allāh سبحانه وتعالى. However, because Qābīl was stingy, he did not give from the best of his wealth. In those days, to show that a sacrifice has been accepted, Allāh سبحانه وتعالى would send a fire storm to take away the sacrifice. When the fire storm had passed by, they noticed that Hābīl's sacrifice was taken away but Qābīl's sacrifice was still where they left it.

When Qābīl realised that his sacrifice was not accepted, instead of seeking forgiveness for his wrong doing, he became very angry. He also started to distrust his father. He accused his father of only making *du'ā'* for Hābīl and not for him, which was not true.[1] It was only an excuse for Qābīl to hide his embarrassment.

[1] Al-Bidāyah wa Al-Nihāyah

Qābīl also became very jealous of his brother. His jealousy and anger grew and grew till he decided to kill his brother.

So Qābīl went to his brother Hābīl in anger and said to him that he was here to kill him! Hābīl explained to his brother that Allāh سبحانه وتعالى only accepts actions from those who fear Allāh سبحانه وتعالى and are sincere. He also said to his brother that he will not harm him because he feared Allāh's سبحانه وتعالى punishment.

Hābīl was kind and loving towards his brother. He hoped that his brother would calm down and not do such a horrible action. Hābīl had a very good heart and responded to his brother's anger in the best of ways; it was a sign of Hābīl's true goodness.

Hābīl also warned his brother of Allāh's سبحانه وتعالى punishment if he killed a human being. The words of Hābīl had an effect on Qābīl; he decided to walk away from such a horrible action. However, this only lasted

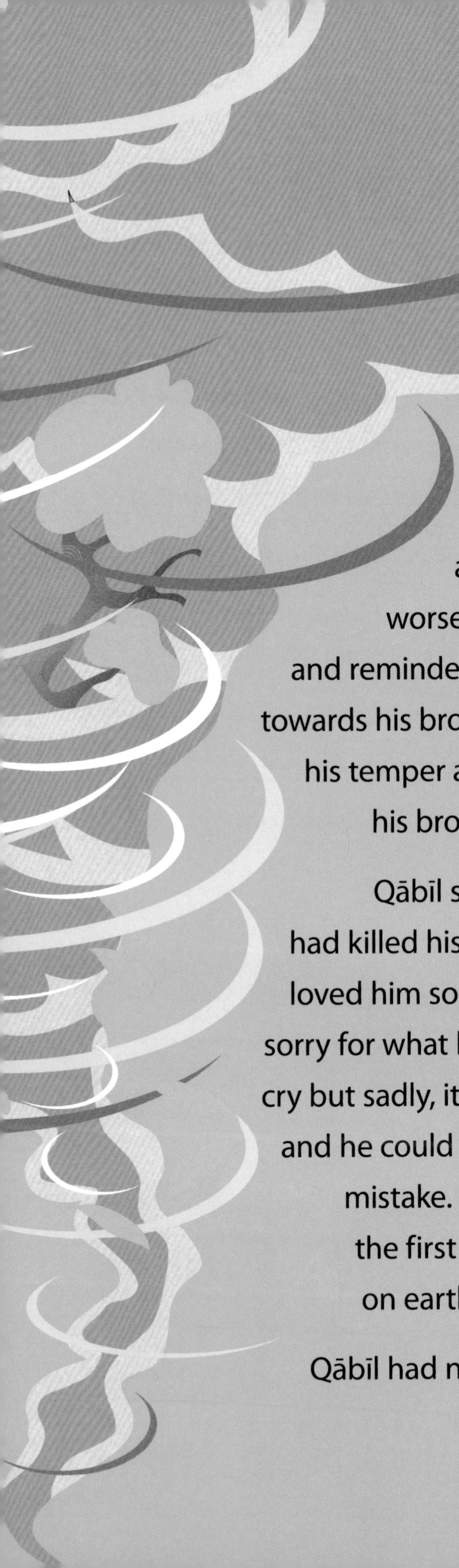

for a short while.

Qābīl kept thinking about what happened; he could not ignore his anger which slowly grew and grew. To make things worse, Shayṭān came to Qābīl and reminded him of the jealousy he felt towards his brother. Once again, Qābīl lost his temper and in a fit of rage, he killed his brother.

Qābīl soon came to his senses; he had killed his beloved brother who had loved him so much. Qābīl felt sad and sorry for what he had done and began to cry but sadly, it was too late. Hābīl was dead and he could not do anything to undo his mistake. Qābīl killing his brother was the first ever murder that happened on earth.

Qābīl had no idea what to do with his

brother's body. Eventually, Allāh سبحانه وتعالى sent a crow that
scratched the ground in search of something. Qābīl
suddenly thought of what to do with the body. He
cried, "O my misery! Could I have not been like this
5:31 crow and covered up my brother's body?!" This made
him even more sad and sorry over his horrible action.
Qābīl dug a hole and buried his brother in the ground.

After mentioning this story in the Qur'ān, Allāh سبحانه وتعالى
follows it with a very important statement. Allāh سبحانه وتعالى
says: "Because of this, We made a law… if anyone kills
a person… it is as if he has killed all of humankind, and
5:32 if anyone saves a life it is as if he has saved the lives of
all humankind." This verse shows us the importance of
another human's life.

Lessons

- We should never be jealous of anyone or become angry. Anger leads to doing things that we later wish we had not done.
- The Prophet صلى الله عليه وسلم warned us that jealousy destroys our good deeds like fire destroys dry wood.[2]
- If someone is angry

and upset towards us, we should remain calm and not respond back with anger. The Prophet ﷺ loved the character of Hābīl and the way he responded to his brother who wanted to kill him. The Prophet ﷺ was asked, "What do you advise a person, towards whom someone has raised their hand to kill?" The Prophet ﷺ replied, "Be like the better son of Ādam."[3]

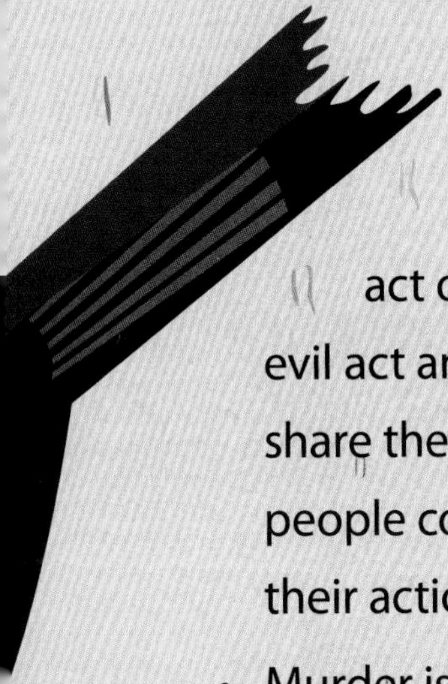

- Prophet Muḥammad ﷺ said: "A soul is not killed out of oppression, except that a portion of [its sin] is on the first son of Ādam, as he was the one who started the act of killing."[4] This teaches us that if we do an evil act and other people copy us then we too, will share the sin. However, if we do a good act and people copy us then we too, will be rewarded for their action.
- Murder is one of the worst sins a human being can commit. Muslims should always try their best to help save and protect lives.

[2] Abū Dāwūd; [3] Aḥmad; [4] Bukhārī

Angels

- Allāh سبحانه وتعالى has created many angels. Only He knows exactly how many angels there are.
- Angels are made from light.
- Unlike us, angels cannot disobey Allāh سبحانه وتعالى.[1]
- They worship Allāh سبحانه وتعالى day and night, and they never get tired.
- They have only been created to serve Allāh سبحانه وتعالى.
- We cannot see angels, but they can see us.
- They do not eat, sleep or drink.
- Allāh سبحانه وتعالى gives each angel its own role. They all carry out many different duties.
- Angels have extraordinary powers.
- Angels are respected servants of Allāh سبحانه وتعالى.
- Angels have no gender. This means that there are no 'male' or 'female' angels.
- Angels can change form and appearance. They can even turn into a human being.
- Angels were created before Ādam عليه السلام.
- Angels have 2, 4, 6 or even 600 wings!
- Some angels are more important than others.

[1] Qur'ān 66:6

The four main angels

Jibrīl عليه السلام brings down Allāh's words to the messengers. He is the greatest angel and has the highest position among them.

Mīkā'īl عليه السلام controls the rain and food. He is in charge of the weather.

Isrāfīl عليه السلام will blow the trumpet twice: First to end the world, and then to start the Day of Judgement.

Malakul Mawt عليه السلام is the Angel of Death. He takes the soul from the body at the time of death.

Respecting people

Muslims respect everyone regardless of who they are and what religion they follow. We should respect everyone no matter what colour they are, where they come from or what language they speak. We should take extra care to show special respect to the following people:

Parents

Parents deserve our special love and respect. When we were small and could not look after ourselves, our parents took care of us. Allāh says in the Qur'ān, "And your Lord has ordered that none should be
17 23 worshipped besides Him, and that goodness should be shown to parents."

The Prophet said, "Paradise is underneath the feet of mothers."[1] About the father he said, "The father is the best door to Paradise."[2]

Elder brothers and sisters

The Prophet said, "The elder brothers have rights over their younger brothers like the rights a father

[1] Aḥmad; [2,5] Tirmidhī

has over his son."[3] The same goes for elder sisters; we should respect them like our mothers and when older brothers and sisters set good examples for us, we should follow their good teachings.

[3] Bayhaqī; [4] Bukhārī; [6,7] Muslim

Aunts and uncles

We should treat them the way we treat our mothers and fathers. They are the brothers and sisters of our parents. Just as we love our brothers and sisters, likewise our parents love their brothers and sisters and would want us to show respect to them. The Prophet صلى الله عليه وسلم said that a person's aunt [mother's sister] is like his own mother.[4]

Teachers

We should show good manners to our teachers at all times and should not be rude to them. We should ask them sensible questions and do things that will please them. A great example of this is the behaviour of Ibn ʿAbbās رضي الله عنه who, as a young boy, went to learn how the Prophet صلى الله عليه وسلم worshipped during the night. As the Prophet صلى الله عليه وسلم went to answer the call of nature, Ibn ʿAbbās رضي الله عنه left a jug of water for him so that he could make *wuḍūʾ* with it. The Prophet صلى الله عليه وسلم was so pleased with this that he made a special *duʿāʾ* for him that Allāh سبحانه وتعالى teaches him the Qurʾān. This *duʿāʾ* was accepted by Allāh سبحانه وتعالى and Ibn ʿAbbās رضي الله عنه became one of the greatest scholars among the Companions.

Elders

We should respect all elders, regardless of their religion. We should care for them, make things easy for them, offer our seat to them, and help them whenever we can. The Prophet ﷺ said, "Whoever does not show respect to our elders and have mercy on our young ones, they do not belong to us."[5]

Neighbours

Neighbours have great importance in Islām. We should never trouble our neighbours in any way. We should always look out for them.

The Prophet ﷺ said, "Jibrīl kept on reminding me of the rights of a neighbour until I began to think that the neighbour would get a share of the family wealth."[6]

One of the rights of the neighbour is that if we have a feast or a party, we should invite them or at the very least, send some food to them.

Islām warns us against treating our neighbours badly. This may even stop us from entering Paradise. The Prophet ﷺ said, "The one whose neighbour is not safe from them, will not enter Paradise."[7]

Books from Allāh

A Muslim must believe in all the Books that Allāh سبحانه وتعالى has sent to his prophets. These books were revealed for the guidance of people. There are four main books that were revealed:

The Tawrāh revealed to Mūsā عليه السلام

Mūsā عليه السلام was the prophet who spoke to Allāh سبحانه وتعالى directly. He had a stick with which he was able to do many miracles. For example, he threw the stick on the ground in front of magicians and it turned into a large snake. Another example is when he threw it in front of a great river and it split in to two.

The Zabūr revealed to Dāwūd عليه السلام

Dāwūd عليه السلام was given the gift of a great voice. The mountains and the birds used to sing hymns along with him. He was also a great king and judge.

The Injīl revealed to ʿĪsā عليه السلام

ʿĪsā عليه السلام was a prophet who Allāh سبحانه وتعالى gave many abilities. He was sent during a time when there were many doctors. These doctors used to cure people, so some people started thinking that Allāh سبحانه وتعالى did not exist. They also believed that there was no life after death. To prove these people wrong, Allāh سبحانه وتعالى gave ʿĪsā عليه السلام the ability to cure the blind and raise the dead back to life.

The Qur'ān revealed to Muḥammad صلى الله عليه وسلم

Muḥammad صلى الله عليه وسلم was sent as a messenger to everyone. Before prophethood, he was known as al-Amīn (the trustworthy). He is the last and final prophet. He was given the Qur'ān as a guidance for all humans until the Day of Judgement. He was also given many miracles.

Unfortunately, all the other books have changed over time. For example, the Bible is not the same as the original Injīl. The Qur'ān is the only book that has not been changed by anyone. Allāh سبحانه وتعالى will never allow anyone to change it. That is why the Qur'ān remains the true book of guidance. It is a living miracle.

Apart from these books, some prophets were given scrolls. These scrolls were smaller than the four holy books and were sent to prophets like Ibrāhīm عليه السلام.

Manners of eating and drinking

Practical lesson

Eating and drinking is an important part of our lives. Allāh ﷻ says in the Qur'ān, "Eat and drink but do not waste; Allāh does not love those who waste". Therefore, eating and drinking can also be a way to earn the same reward as worshipping Allāh ﷻ. We earn this reward when we eat and drink by copying the ways of our Prophet ﷺ.

7 31

When eating or drinking we should:

- Say, "*Bismillāh,*"[1] before we start. By doing this, Allāh ﷻ will bless our food and drink.
- Use the right hand.
- Sit down.
- Look at what we are eating or drinking.
- Say, "*Alḥamdulillāh,*"[2] when we finish.

When eating we should:

- Wash our hands before and after eating.

- Eat from the side of the plate that is closest to us.
- Eat in a way that others do not find unpleasant.
- Not complain or find faults in the food.
- Not blow on the food if it is hot, but allow it to cool by itself.
- Finish what is on our plates as well as what is left on our fingers, for we do not know which part of the food is blessed.

When drinking we should:

- Drink by taking small sips and not large gulps.
- Not drink in one go, but take three turns (between each turn, we should take a breath, but not breathe into our drink).
- Drink from a glass or cup and not directly from the bottle or jug.

Our Prophet ﷺ would sit with others when eating and loved to share his food with others. He would even eat from the same plate. We too, should do the same.

[1,2] Full *du'ā's* are in Safar Du'ā' Book 1

Prophets of Allāh

Prophets have been sent to different people so they can guide them to Allāh سبحانه وتعالى. Allāh سبحانه وتعالى made them perfect examples for their people. All prophets were:

Intelligent

All prophets were very intelligent. When the Kaʿbah was being rebuilt and the Black Stone needed to be placed back into the Kaʿbah, an argument took place between the Quraysh. Prophet Muḥammad صلى الله عليه وسلم came up with a solution. He told them to place the stone on a piece of cloth and for each leader to hold a corner of the cloth and he placed the stone in the Kaʿbah.

Sinless

Prophets and messengers can never commit sin. Even before they became prophets, they never committed any sins.

When our Prophet (صلى الله عليه وسلم) was a teenager, he decided to go with some people to an event where there was a lot of music and dancing. Allāh (سبحانه وتعالى) protected him from this sin by making him fall into a deep sleep. When he awoke, the festival was over.

Truthful

Prophets were always honest and never told a lie, because lying is a sin. Prophet Muḥammad (صلى الله عليه وسلم) was known as aṣ-Ṣādiq (the Truthful) even before Allāh (سبحانه وتعالى) had revealed the Qur'ān to him.

Obedient

Prophets were always obedient to Allāh (سبحانه وتعالى) and never disobeyed Him.

Allāh (سبحانه وتعالى) tested his prophets to show us how obedient they were and they always passed the test. He told Ibrāhīm (عليه السلام) to sacrifice his son Ismāʿīl (عليه السلام) and both of them obeyed Allāh (سبحانه وتعالى). But Allāh (سبحانه وتعالى) was only testing them, so he replaced Ismāʿīl (عليه السلام) with a ram. The ram was sacrificed and Ismāʿīl (عليه السلام) was spared.

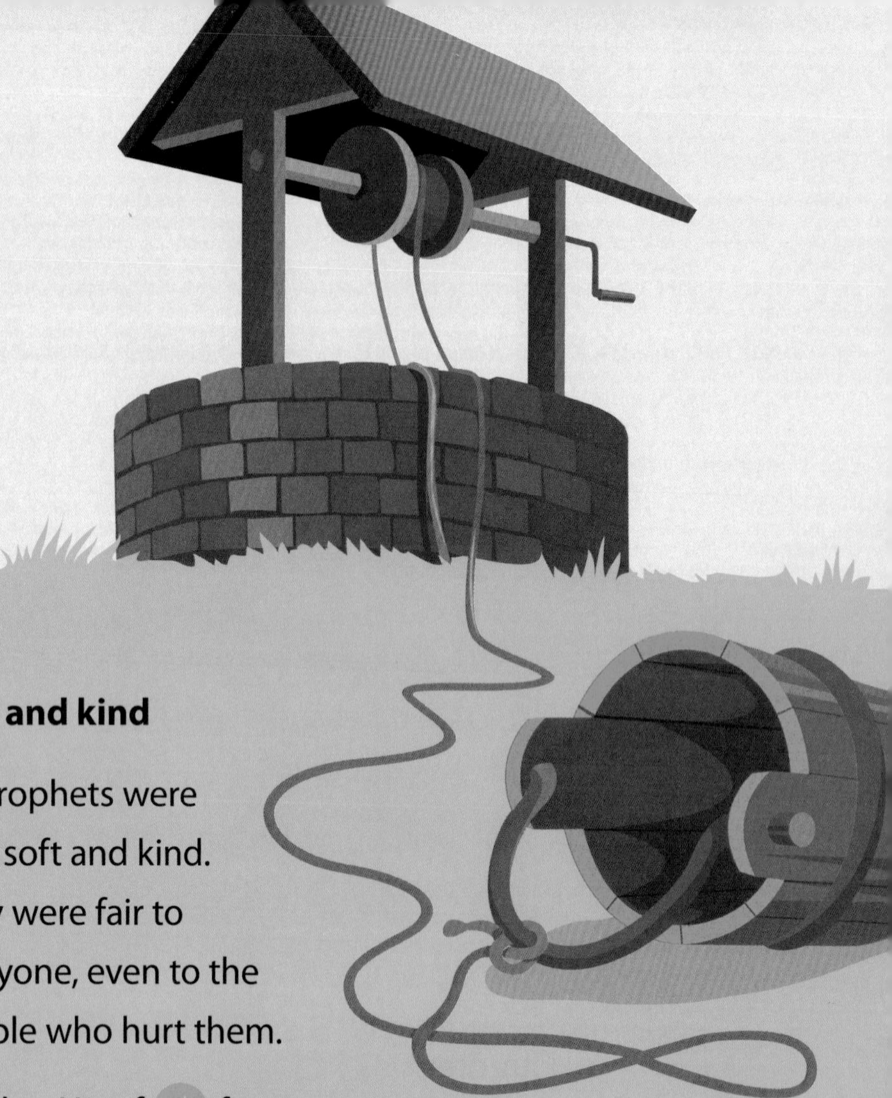

Soft and kind

All Prophets were very soft and kind. They were fair to everyone, even to the people who hurt them.

Prophet Yūsuf (عليه السلام) forgave his brothers even though they left him inside a deep well when he was young. He could have died in the well. Their father, Prophet Yaʿqūb (عليه السلام), also forgave his children for what they did.

When prophets came, people knew they had the best actions and character. The last prophet Allāh (سبحانه وتعالى) sent to this world was Prophet Muḥammad (صلى الله عليه وسلم). There are no more prophets after him.

Life after death

People will be sweating according to their sins. Some will be sweating up to their ankles, some up to their knees and some will be drowning.

The Day of Judgement is a day when all humans and jinns will have to stand in front of Allāh سبحانه وتعالى. Everyone will be reminded about the things they did in the world. Those who did good deeds will be rewarded and those who did bad deeds may be punished.

- The day will be 50,000 years long.
- The sun will be directly above peoples' heads, and it will be a very difficult day for some people.
- Some people will be so worried about themselves that they will even run away from their loved ones.

There are different stages in the Hereafter:

The Grave

When Muslims die they are buried in a grave. Inside the grave, the soul is returned back to the body so that it can be questioned.

Two angels, Munkar and Nakīr عليهم السلام, are sent to the grave. They ask the person three questions:

1. "Who is your Lord?"
2. "What is your religion?"
3. "Who is this man [Prophet Muḥammad صلى الله عليه وسلم]?"

For those who answer the questions correctly, their graves will become as wide as the eye can see. Also, a door to Paradise will open, and a cool, beautiful breeze from Paradise will blow through it. The grave will be a place of peace and rest for them.

Who is your Lord?

For those who cannot answer the questions, the graves will become so narrow that it will squeeze them together. Like this, people will stay in their graves until Allāh سبحانه وتعالى raises them on the Day of Judgement.

What is your religion?

Rising from the graves

After many years, Allāh سبحانه وتعالى will bring everyone back to life from their graves. Everyone, from the first person to the last person, will come back to life.

Who is this man?

The Gathering

Everyone will be gathered in one big place. Then the good people and the bad people will be separated from each other. Everyone will be sweating according to their sins because of the closeness of the Sun. Some people will be sweating up to their ankles, some up to their knees and others will be drowning in their sweat. Some special people will not be sweating at all but will be under the shade of the Throne of Allāh سبحانه وتعالى.

The Questioning

Allāh سبحانه وتعالى will show people all the good and bad deeds they did in the world. Even deeds which are as small as a seed will be shown. Everyone will be judged fairly. The good and bad deeds will be weighed on the Scale.

The Book of Deeds

Everything we do and say in our life is written down by angels in our Book of Deeds. On the Day of Judgement, we will be shown our Book of Deeds. Those who receive their Book of Deeds in their right hand will go to Paradise. The people who receive their Book of Deeds in their left hand will be punished.

Paradise

Jannah (Paradise) is a place full of beautiful gardens. Allāh سبحانه وتعالى has made Paradise for people who do good.

- People can do whatever they want in Paradise.
- There will be palaces made from gold and silver.
- There will be many beautiful gardens with shady trees and different types of rivers.
- Everyone will be happy. There will be no sadness.
- Enjoyment in Paradise will always keep on increasing.
- No one will ever die in Paradise.

The smallest garden in Paradise is 10 times bigger than the world we live in.

Think of all the things you can have and do in Paradise. You can have a flying car, or you can even fly yourself. You can have a chocolate river which goes through your bedroom. You can invite lots of friends to your palace and play games all the time. You can do amazing things like jump off a very high mountain and bounce back up.

Hell

Jahannam (Hell) is also known as al-Nār, the Fire. The Qurʾān warns us about Jahannam; it is not a place of happiness or ease. Allāh says in the Qurʾān, "Those who do not believe in Our verses [of the Qurʾān], We shall send them to the Fire..." People who do very bad deeds and do not ask Allāh for forgiveness may also be sent to Hell unless Allāh forgives them. 4 56

The Prophet taught us that whoever believes in Allāh and in Muḥammad as His Messenger, will be saved from Jahannam.[1] He also taught us to save ourselves from Jahannam by doing good actions.[2]

Think of what may happen to us if we end up in Jahannam. Everything we are afraid of will be there. It is a place of sadness and loneliness.

This is why we should always think about our actions and behaviour. We should always do good deeds. We should make *duʿāʾ* to Allāh to save us from Hell and let us into Paradise. If you think you did something bad you should say, "O Allāh, I ask you to forgive me; I won't do it again," and Allāh will forgive you.

[1] Tirmidhī [2] Bukhārī and Muslim

Prophet Hūd and the people of ʿĀd

Many years after the great flood of Nūḥ عليه السلام, there lived a group of people called ʿĀd. They lived in a city called Iram, which was known as the City of Thousand Pillars. It was somewhere between Yemen and Oman.

Allāh سبحانه وتعالى had blessed them with great strength and size; they were actually giants! He blessed them with many children, wealth and animals that lived in beautiful gardens and springs. They were also known for being very good craftsmen and they made tall and beautiful buildings. They were very proud of these gifts and believed no one was greater than them.

Instead of ʿĀd being grateful to Allāh سبحانه وتعالى and thanking Him, they started to create idols. They turned to the idols asking for help and also began to worship them. They had forgotten how Allāh سبحانه وتعالى punished the people of Nūḥ عليه السلام with the flood. Their strength and wealth made them arrogant.

Allāh سبحانه وتعالى did not destroy ʿĀd straightaway but sent a prophet to guide them. This prophet was Hūd عليه السلام who belonged to their tribe. He was a very patient and good person.

An arrogant person behaves in a proud and unpleasant way towards others because they believe they are more important than them.

He called out to his people, asking them to remember that it was only Allāh سبحانه وتعالى who had given them the blessings they enjoyed. He told them to worship Allāh سبحانه وتعالى alone and not to worship anything else.

However, they mocked him saying, "Are you after money?" He replied, "My people, I do not ask you for money; my reward is only with Allāh." He told them about life after death and what might happen to them. They laughed saying, “How can we be brought back to life after we become dust and bones?!”

He argued that these idols could neither cause harm nor benefit. He also reminded them about the people of Nūḥ عليه السلام but his people called him foolish and said that their gods were punishing him with this madness. They even boasted, “Who can be stronger than us!” but little did they think that Allāh سبحانه وتعالى who created them in the first place, was surely stronger than them.

Finally, tired of hearing the message of Hūd عليه السلام and his warnings, his people demanded, “So where is this punishment and when will it come?!” He told them that only Allāh سبحانه وتعالى knows such a thing. They replied, “We shall wait for the punishment!” Hūd عليه السلام was saddened by their behaviour and wished they accepted the truth.

Soon after, the people of ʿĀd faced difficulties because of a drought. The sky no longer sent rain while the sun burnt the land. Because there was little water, their beautiful gardens and land became dry and their crops and animals started dying. When Hūd عليه السلام told them it was a punishment from Allāh سبحانه وتعالى they did not believe him.

Finally a huge, dark, black cloud appeared. The people of ʿĀd were very happy to see this, "This cloud will give us rain!" they cried out in joy. However, to their surprise, this cloud turned in to a very strong wind. It was so strong that it lifted the trees from the ground. The mighty wind travelled

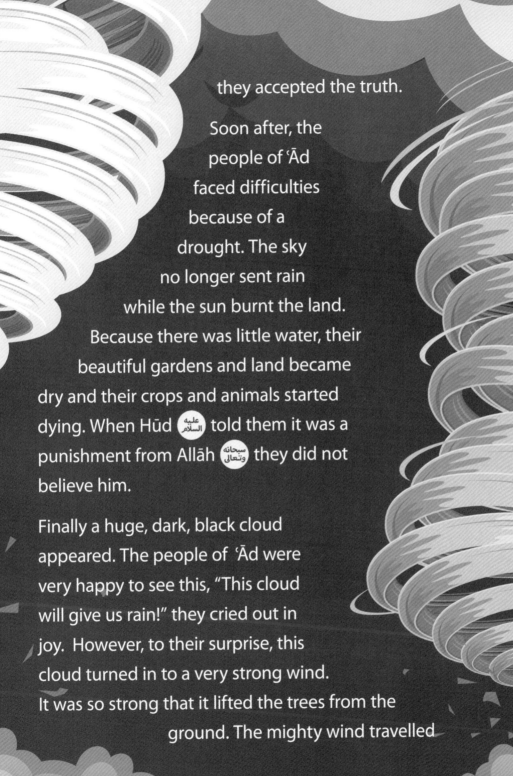

through the city destroying everything in its path. It threw the giants of ʿĀd on to the ground so hard that their bodies were left in pieces across the land. They were never to rise and boast again. This storm continued for seven nights and eight days.[1]

Hūd عليه السلام and those few who believed in his message were saved. They had travelled to Ḥaḍramawt, which is in Yemen and worshipped Allāh سبحانه وتعالى there peacefully.

Lessons

- We should always be grateful for the things Allāh سبحانه وتعالى has given us.
- Nobody is more powerful than Allāh سبحانه وتعالى.
- We should never be arrogant. Allāh سبحانه وتعالى does not like arrogant and proud people.
- The strength of the nation of ʿĀd could not save them, even though they were giants.
- Allāh's سبحانه وتعالى punishment is very serious. We must always ask Allāh سبحانه وتعالى for His forgiveness whenever we do anything wrong.
- Allāh سبحانه وتعالى will always look after the people who believe in the message He sends.

[1] Qur'ān 69:7

Cleanliness

Cleanliness is an important part of a Muslim's life. A Muslim cannot do any prayers or any other act of worship without it. Allāh سبحانه وتعالى says that He loves those who are clean and pure. This is why Muslims should always be clean and wear clean clothes.

The Prophet صلى الله عليه وسلم said, "Keeping clean is half of faith."[1] Therefore, Muslims should keep clean at all times.

Cleanliness is not only wearing clean clothes, it is also doing *wuḍū'* and *ghusl* regularly. The Prophet صلى الله عليه وسلم used to like wearing clean clothes and putting on nice perfume.

We must perform *wuḍū'* before praying *Ṣalāh* or touching the Qur'ān. We must make sure our bodies and clothes are clean, and then perform *wuḍū'*. The Prophet صلى الله عليه وسلم said, "The key to Paradise is prayer and the key to prayer is *wuḍū'*."[2]

Apart from this, we should also come to the *masjid* with nice clothes because we are going to the house of Almighty Allāh سبحانه وتعالى, who is the King of all kings.

[1] Muslim; [2] Tirmidhī

Manners of using the toilet

Extra care needs to be taken when using the toilet, as the toilet can be an unclean place. If the toilet is used the way the Prophet ﷺ taught us, we will be rewarded. However, if we do not use it properly we may be punished. Our Prophet ﷺ has warned us saying, "One of the main reasons for a person being punished in the grave is because of [not being careful when passing] urine."[1]

Follow the rules below when using the toilet:

1. Take your socks off before entering the toilet to keep them clean. The floor or slippers may have

[1] Aḥmad

urine on it or be unclean.

2. Recite the *duʿāʾ* below before entering the toilet:

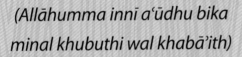

اَللّٰهُمَّ اِنِّيْ اَعُوْذُبِكَ مِنَ الْخُبُثِ
وَالْخَبَائِثِ

(Allāhumma innī aʿūdhu bika minal khubuthi wal khabāʾith)

3. Enter the toilet with the left foot. And before sitting down, check that there is water and toilet tissue.
4. If the toilet seat is not clean, wipe it before sitting down. This can be done with wet tissue.
5. Inside the toilet, do not talk, recite any Qurʾān, say any *duʿāʾ* or mention Allāh سبحانه وتعالى or the Prophet's صلى الله عليه وسلم name.

6. After finishing, wipe the private parts with tissue and then wash with water where available (if there is no tissue, water will be enough). Hold the water jug with the right hand and wash the private parts with the left hand.

> The Prophet ﷺ said, "One of the main reasons for a person being punished in the grave is because of [not being careful when passing] urine."

7. Wipe the seat with tissue to ensure it is clean and flush the toilet. Always leave the toilet in a way you would like to find it.
8. Remember to wash your hands when you have finished. Exit the toilet with your right foot then recite the following *du'ā'*:

غُفْرَانَكَ ، اَلْحَمْدُ لِلّٰهِ الَّذِيْ أَذْهَبَ عَنِّي الأَذٰى وَعَافَانِيْ

(Ghufrānaka, alḥamdu lillāhil ladhī adhhaba 'annil adhā wa 'āfānī)

Boys and girls should sit to use the toilet. If you stand up and use the toilet, you will most likely make the seat or your clothes unclean with urine. If you leave urine on the toilet seat and it gets onto somebody else's body or clothes, you will be sinful for doing so.

Why Muslims perform Ṣalāh

Virtues of praying *Ṣalāh*

- *Ṣalāh* is the second pillar of Islām.[1]
- *Ṣalāh* is a key to Paradise.[2]
- *Ṣalāh* stops us from doing bad deeds.[3]
- *Du'ā'* made after *Ṣalāh* is accepted.[4]

Abū Dharr رضي الله عنه said that once the Prophet صلى الله عليه وسلم came outside in autumn while the leaves were falling off the trees. Abū Dharr رضي الله عنه said, "The Prophet took hold of a branch of a tree and shook it until all its leaves began to fall. At this he said, 'O Abū Dharr!' I replied, 'At your service O Messenger of Allāh.' He said, 'When a Muslim prays *Ṣalāh* to please Allāh, his sins fall off from him just as these leaves fell off this tree.'"[5]

Later on, Salmān رضي الله عنه, who was a friend of the Prophet صلى الله عليه وسلم, would do exactly the same with a branch to remind people of what the Prophet صلى الله عليه وسلم had said.[6]

Warnings on missing Ṣalāh

- It is a major sin to knowingly miss *Ṣalāh,* or not perform *Ṣalāh* because of laziness.
- Allāh سبحانه وتعالى has no responsibility toward a person who misses *Ṣalāh* intentionally.[7]
- When a person misses a *Ṣalāh*, it is as though they have lost everything.[8]
- Missing *Ṣalāh* may lead to more sins and other bad actions.

Anas رضي الله عنه narrated that the Prophet صلى الله عليه وسلم said, "A person who prays his *Ṣalāh* on time and performs *wuḍū'*, *qiyām*, *rukū'* and *sajdah* properly, his *Ṣalāh* appears bright and beautiful. The *Ṣalāh* says to the person, 'May Allāh look after you just as you have looked after me.' The person who does not pray his *Ṣalāh* on time nor does he perform *wuḍū'*, *qiyām*, *rukū'* or *sajdah* properly, his *Ṣalāh* appears dark and ugly. The *Ṣalāh* says to the person, 'May Allāh ruin you just as you have ruined me.' Then, that *Ṣalāh* is wrapped up like an old piece of cloth and thrown at the person's face."[9]

[1] Bukhārī; [2,4] Tirmidhī; [3] Qur'ān 29:45; [5,6,7,8] Aḥmad; [9] Ṭabarānī

Revision of rak'ahs

Practical lesson

First cycle

1	2	3	4	5	6	7	8
Intention	*Takbīr*	Standing	*Rukū'*	Stand up	*Sajdah*	Sitting	Second *sajdah*

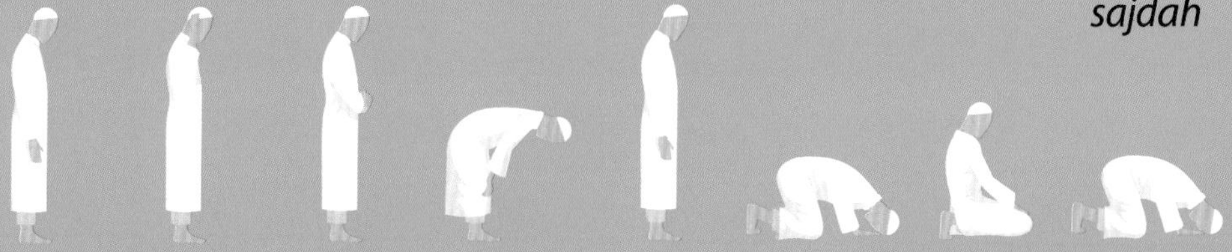

Second cycle

9	10	11	12	13	14	15
Standing	*Rukū'*	Stand up	*Sajdah*	Sitting	Second *sajdah*	Last sitting

▾ or ▸

End with *salām* to complete a two *rak'ah* prayer, or continue.

Third cycle

16	17	18	19	20	21	22
Standing	*Rukū'*	Stand up	*Sajdah*	Sitting	Second *sajdah*	Last sitting

▾ or ▸

End with *salām* for three *rak'ah*, or skip step 22 and continue.

Fourth cycle

23	24	25	26	27	28	29
Standing	*Rukū'*	Stand up	*Sajdah*	Sitting	Second *sajdah*	Last sitting

End with *salām* to complete a prayer with four *rak'ah* cycles.

The companions in the cave

About 400 years after ʿĪsā عليه السلام, there was an Emperor who was very cruel. His name was Decius and he ruled the great Roman Empire, which stretched from Spain to the Persian Gulf. Like some people before him, he also began to worship idols. He forced the people in his empire to follow him in worshipping idols too. They had a god of war, the goddess of love, the sun-god, the god of the oceans and many many others. People were forced to praise and honour these statues, otherwise they faced punishment. The people included many good Christians who had believed in the only true God, Allāh سبحانه وتعالى, and they believed in ʿĪsā عليه السلام as His Messenger. However, the Emperor did not want the people to believe in Allāh سبحانه وتعالى or His Messenger, ʿĪsā عليه السلام.

Within the Roman Empire, there was a city called Ephesus near the Mediterranean Sea. It was a busy city with a great port. Traders from all over the Empire came to buy and sell their goods there. In this city, there lived a group of brave young boys, who all believed in the one true God, Allāh سبحانه وتعالى. They had never worshipped idols, and they would always pray to Allāh سبحانه وتعالى for help and guidance. Allāh سبحانه وتعالى answered their prayers and gave them strength in their hearts. Because of this, they were not afraid of revealing their belief in the truth to the people that they lived with.

People were forced to honour and praise statues or face punishment.

The brave young boys

One day, the young boys went to the marketplace and stood up on a platform so all the people around them could see and hear them. They cried out, "Our Lord is the Lord of the heavens and the earth. We shall never turn to any god other than Him because if we did, it would surely be a lie!" The crowd suddenly stopped what they were doing and turned to the boys who had so bravely made their belief known. A lot of people in the crowd agreed and even believed in what the young boys said. Unfortunately, they were too afraid of going against the Emperor because whenever they mentioned Allāh سبحانه وتعالى they were punished.

However, the brave young boys were not scared and carried on with their message saying, "These people of
18 15 ours have taken up gods other than Allāh. Why do they not bring a clear proof? And who is more unfair than the one who makes up a lie against Allāh?"

When the Emperor heard of them trying to get people to change their beliefs, he called for the boys and questioned them about what they worshipped. They told him that they worshipped Allāh سبحانه وتعالى alone and they did not make any partners with Him. The Emperor was angry at their response. He gave them three days to change their faith. He threatened to kill them if they did not worship idols like everyone else.

The cave

The young boys, fearing for their life, ran away to a cave high up in a mountain, outside of the city. On their way to the cave, a dog followed them. It did not leave their side even though they tried to chase it away.

18 10 As the brave young boys hid in the cave they prayed, "Our Lord, bless us with mercy from Yourself and guide us in this problem of ours." Now, after finding safety in the cave, the young boys were very tired from all the running. They all fell into a deep sleep. The dog sat at the entrance with its front legs stretched out and eyes wide open. Allāh سبحانه وتعالى protected the young boys because anyone who passed by the cave saw the fierce-looking dog and ran away.

When they finally woke up, one of them asked, "How long did we sleep?" Some of them thought they had only slept for a day or part of a day. Others said, "Allah knows best," but one thing was for sure; they were all very hungry. They decided that one of them should go to the city with money and buy some food. They told him to be very careful so that no one realises who he is. They also told

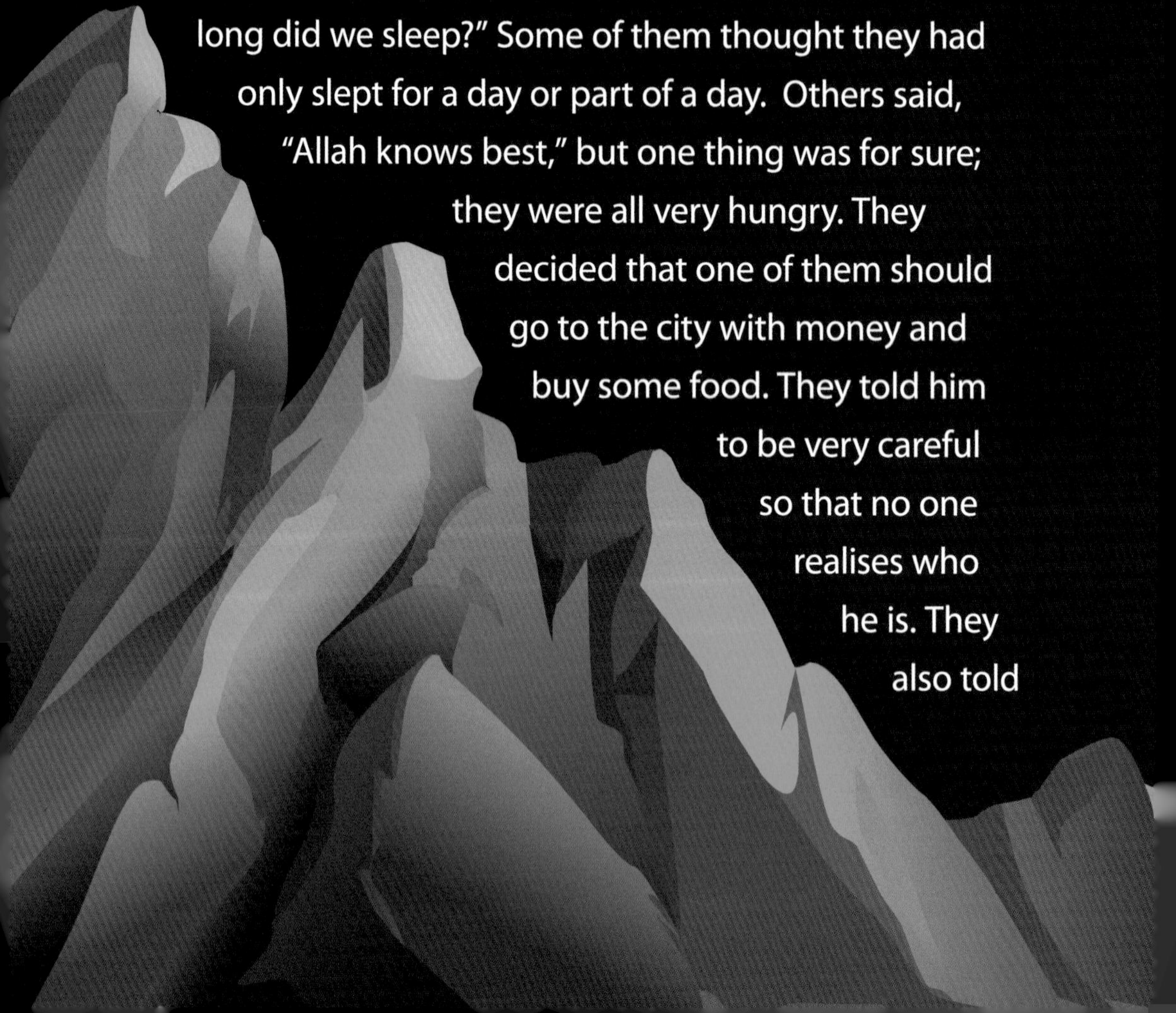

him that he should not tell anyone about the rest of his friends hiding in the cave.

Back to the market

The young boy made his way to the city of Ephesus with some money in his pocket. As he entered the city, he noticed that things seemed strange. The people were all wearing unusual clothes. The buildings looked different. Even the people looked different. As he walked around the city, he was unable to recognise anyone. He was surprised at how much the city had changed in just a few hours.

He went to the market and found a shop selling food. When the young boy took out his money to pay, the shopkeeper was surprised to see the coins he was handed. He showed the coin to the shopkeeper beside him and like this, the coin got passed around many different stalls. They all thought the young boy had found some treasure. “Where did you get this from?”

he asked. "I had it in my pocket from yesterday," replied the boy, wondering what was going on. "This money has been out of date for over 300 years!," said the shopkeeper.

The boy was shocked at the shopkeeper's comment. People in the market started crowding around him. He now realised what had happened. Allāh سبحانه وتعالى had saved him and his companions from the punishment of the evil Emperor, by making them sleep for over 300 years! When he told everyone about what had happened, people were absolutely amazed. He was told that the whole city had changed and the people became believers of Allāh سبحانه وتعالى.

The wicked ruler, Decius, had died long ago and now a new Emperor, who was very good, ruled over the land. The whole city came out of their houses and marched with the new Emperor to the cave where the other young boys were. They had all heard an old story of some young boys who had fled during the rule of Decius to escape death and were never found.

Through this great event, Allāh سبحانه وتعالى taught some

important lessons to the people. Afterwards, Allāh سبحانه وتعالى made the young boys pass away, just as He had made them to sleep for over 300 years. The new Emperor then ordered a place of worship for Allāh سبحانه وتعالى to be built near the cave.

Lessons

- When Muslims remain strong, Allāh سبحانه وتعالى will always help them.
- Allāh سبحانه وتعالى taught this story so young people know that He is with them if they are truthful.
- It is not only through prophets that Allāh سبحانه وتعالى shows His extraordinary powers. He also shows it through ordinary people that are close to Him.
- Time is in Allāh's سبحانه وتعالى control. He can make a long amount of time seem very short and a short amount of time seem very long.
- The story reminds us of how Allāh سبحانه وتعالى will bring people back to life after death.

Manners of the masjid

Practical lesson

The *masjid* is the house of Allāh سبحانه وتعالى. Therefore, we must treat the *masjid* with the highest level of respect and care.

One of the rights of the *masjid* is that we go to it for the five daily prayers - especially men and boys - because the reward is multiplied by 27 times. Women and girls may also perform *Ṣalāh* in the *masjid* but they will also get a lot of reward for performing *Ṣalāh* at home.

We should go to the *masjid* wearing our best and cleanest clothes. We should wear such clothes that are fit to meet the King of all kings. Angels do not like the smells that people do not like; this means, they do not like bad breath, smelly clothes or smelly socks.

We place our shoes on the racks or in such a way that nobody can trip over them. We enter the *masjid* with our right foot and read the *du'ā'*:

اَللّٰهُمَّ افْتَحْ لِيْ أَبْوَابَ رَحْمَتِكْ

(Allāhummaf taḥlī abwāba raḥmatik)

"O Allāh open the doors of your mercy for me"

Before we sit down in the *masjid*, if it we are able to, we should perform two *rak'ah* of prayer. This prayer is known as *Taḥiyyatul masjid*, which means 'The prayer to greet the *masjid*'

When we glorify Allāh سبحانه وتعالى we say words to show how excellent He is, like the word *Subḥānallāh*.

When we are in the *masjid*, we should not disturb others. Even if others break this rule, we should not do the same. Rather, we should remain busy in remembering Allāh سبحانه وتعالى, reading the Qur'ān or glorifying and praising Him. We should try our best not to talk about anything that has no benefit in this world or the next life.

If we find anything unclean or messy in the *masjid*, we should clean it because

there is great reward in doing this. During the time of the Prophet ﷺ, when a woman who used to clean the Prophet's ﷺ *masjid* died, the Prophet ﷺ saw her standing in Paradise with the dust of the *masjid* in her hand.[1] He also warned us that one of the worst sins is when something dirty in the *masjid* is not cleaned.

The *mu'adhdhin* makes the call to prayer.

The *imam* leads the people in prayer.

We should respect all people who come to the *masjid*, especially the *imām*, the *mu'adhdhin* and even the cleaner.

If we read a book or Qur'ān in the *masjid*, we should put it back in the same place where we found it. We should never take anything home that belongs to the *masjid*. Finally, when we decide to leave the *masjid*, we exit with our left foot first, saying:

اَللّٰهُمَّ إِنِّي أَسْئَلُكَ مِنْ فَضْلِكْ

(Allāhumma innī as'aluka min faḍlik)

"O Allāh! I ask You for Your favours."

[1] Bukhārī

Prophet Ṣāliḥ and the people of Thamūd

After Allāh سبحانه وتعالى destroyed the people of ʿĀd, there came the people of Thamūd. They lived in the valleys in Arabia. Like ʿĀd, Thamūd were also giants. They carved out houses in the mountains and made huge castles. They were very proud of the place they lived in because it had beautiful gardens, full of fruits and springs of fresh water. However, just like the people before them, Shayṭān tricked them in believing that idols had given them all of these great blessings.

Thamūd were giants who carved out houses for themselves in the mountains.

Shayṭān also made them feel so proud of their great strength that slowly, they became cruel towards other people.

Allāh سبحانه وتعالى sent Prophet Ṣāliḥ عليه السلام to guide the people of Thamūd. Ṣāliḥ عليه السلام was a good and honest person. He told them not to worship anyone but Allāh سبحانه وتعالى.[1] He also reminded them that Allāh سبحانه وتعالى was the only true God, and that He had given them their mighty strength and blessed them with beautiful lands.

He also reminded them of how Allāh سبحانه وتعالى had destroyed the people of ʿĀd because they were proud and did not listen to Prophet Hūd عليه السلام. He asked them to seek forgiveness and warned them that if they did not, Allāh سبحانه وتعالى would punish them too.

Unfortunately, only a few people believed him. Most of them turned away from Ṣāliḥ عليه السلام. They said, "Before this, we had a lot of hope in you Ṣāliḥ! Are you trying to stop us worshipping the gods our fathers worshipped? We have a lot of doubt in what you are saying!"

[1] Qur'ān 7:74

The great camel

Ṣāliḥ عليه السلام remained strong in calling them to Allāh سبحانه وتعالى but his people became fed up with him. To prove him wrong, they asked Ṣāliḥ عليه السلام to do something they thought he could not do; they asked him for a miracle. Ṣāliḥ عليه السلام made them promise that if he did what they asked, they would all become believers.

Pointing to a great rock, they asked Ṣāliḥ عليه السلام to bring out a red she-camel with a ten month old baby camel in its stomach. Ṣāliḥ عليه السلام reminded them of their promise and then made *du'ā'* to Allāh سبحانه وتعالى to carry out this miracle.

So, Allāh سبحانه وتعالى brought out a camel from the rock right before their eyes. The people of Thamūd were shocked to see this miracle come true. However, after seeing the incredible camel, only a few kept their promise and believed in Ṣāliḥ's عليه السلام message. Most of them still rejected him and called him a magician. They claimed the camel was just a magic trick.

This she-camel was much larger than all the other camels. It needed a lot of water to drink. Whenever this camel came to drink from the well, none of the other animals were able to drink because they were afraid of its size. The people did not like this so they complained to Ṣāliḥ عليه السلام. They finally agreed with Ṣāliḥ عليه السلام that the camel would drink from the well one day and the other animals would drink from it the next day.[2] Ṣāliḥ عليه السلام also warned them not to harm the she-camel because if they did, Allāh سبحانه وتعالى would punish them.

An evil plan and the punishment

The people of Thamūd did not like the camel because it proved Allāh سبحانه وتعالى was true and their gods were false. They wanted to get rid of it, so they planned to kill it. One day, a group of them followed it to the well, and one of them fired an arrow at the camel's leg. This hurt the camel and made it weak; the camel was now unable to run away. Then, they killed it.

After killing the camel, they mocked Ṣāliḥ عليه السلام. They dared him, "If you are a prophet, bring us the punishment!" Ṣāliḥ عليه السلام warned them saying, "Enjoy your time for three more days, then the punishment will fall on you."[3] Also, nine big leaders, who were the worst of them, held a secret meeting, in which they

[2] Qur'ān 26:155; [3] Qur'ān 7:77

said, “Let’s go and kill Ṣāliḥ عليه السلام and his whole family. We will then lie to everyone and say we did not see anything!”[4]

However, Allāh سبحانه وتعالى also had a plan. When three days had passed, He made Ṣāliḥ عليه السلام and his followers leave the area. Allāh سبحانه وتعالى then struck the people of Thamūd with thunderbolts. He also caused a big earthquake to shake the land violently. Then, a horrible scream destroyed Thamūd. Their mighty houses did not save them and no traces of them were left behind. It was as though they had never existed at all.

The strong houses of Thamūd could not save them from the punishment of Allāh سبحانه وتعالى.

Lessons

- We should take lessons from what happened to people in the past and not commit the same sins and mistakes they did.
- We should not be cruel to people, especially if Allāh سبحانه وتعالى has given us more strength or power.
- Prophets are sent to guide people to good.
- Allāh سبحانه وتعالى has power to do everything. He made a living thing (the she-camel) come out of something not living (a rock).

[4] Qur’ān 27:48

Daily Ṣalāh: theory

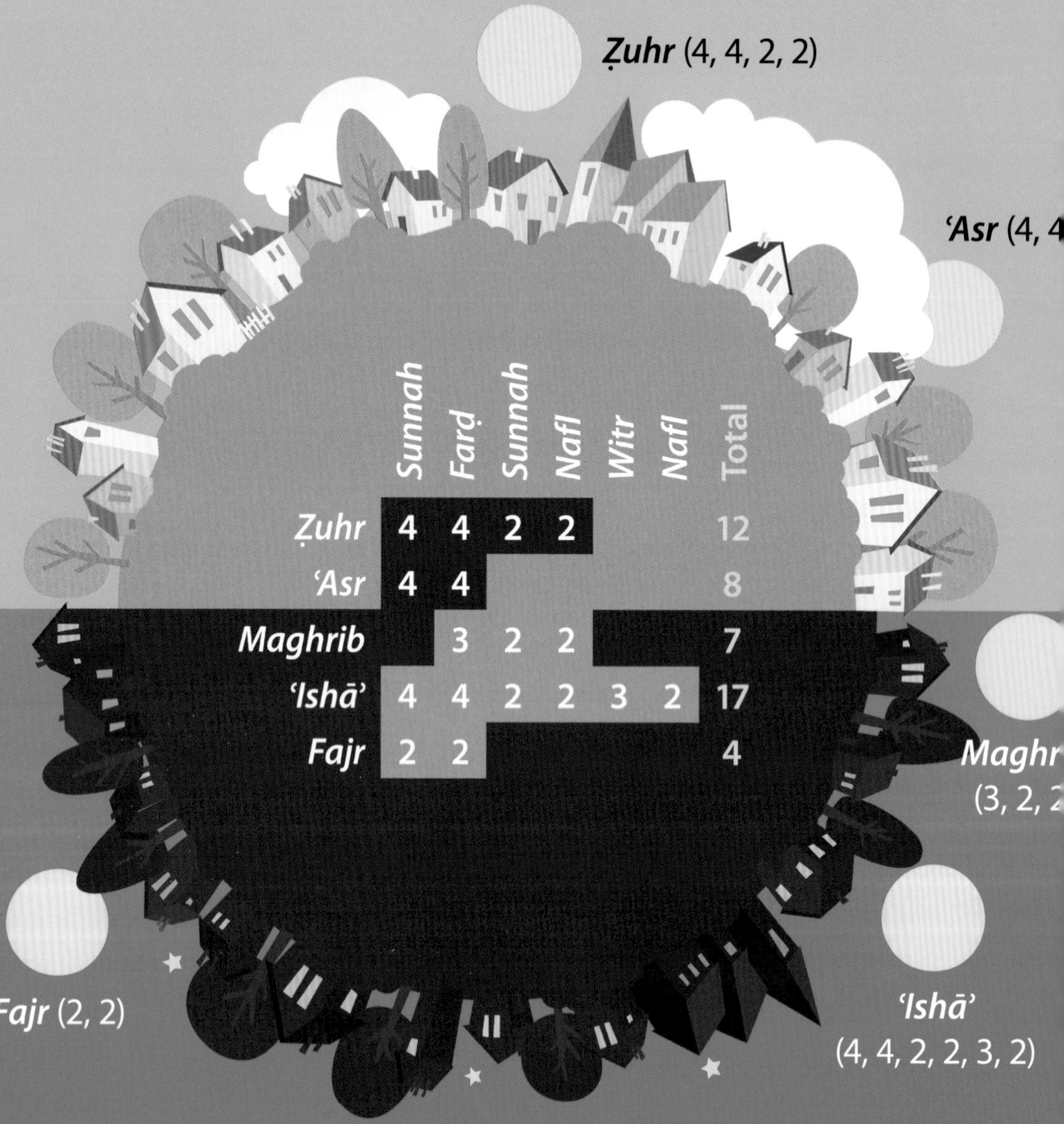

	Sunnah	*Farḍ*	*Sunnah*	*Nafl*	*Witr*	*Nafl*	Total
Ẓuhr	4	4	2	2			12
‘Asr	4	4					8
Maghrib		3	2	2			7
‘Ishā’	4	4	2	2	3	2	17
Fajr	2	2					4

Prophet Shuʿayb and the people of Madyan

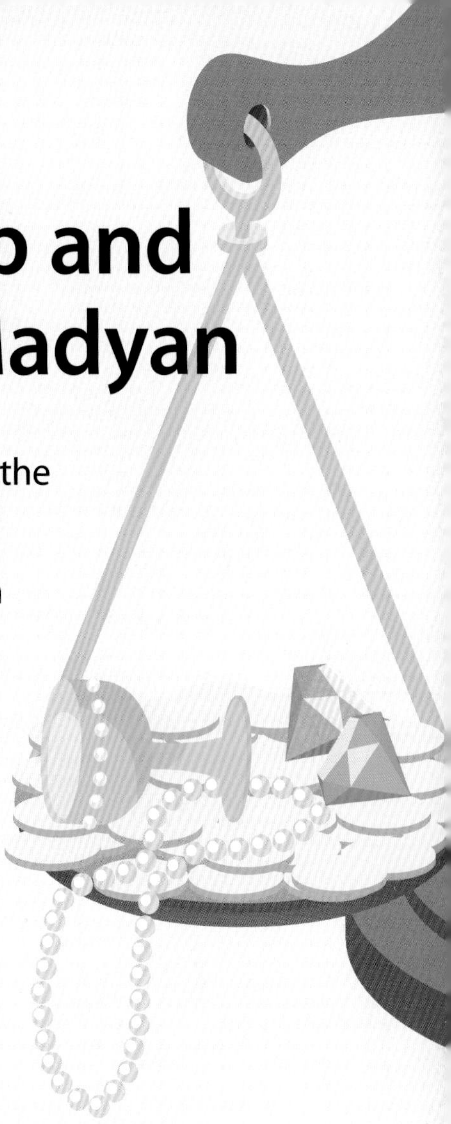

Allāh سبحانه وتعالى sent Prophet Shuʿayb عليه السلام to the people of Madyan. A lot of traders and caravans used to pass through Madyan and over time, this made the city a rich place to live.

The people of Madyan were businessmen who loved making money. Unfortunately, they were also very greedy. In those days, they used scales to measure goods when buying or selling. The greedy businessmen used to cheat others when using the scales. Whatever they owed others, they would always give less. Whatever others owed them, they would always take more than what they deserved.[1]

Also, if there were any faults in their goods, they would hide them and

[1] Qur'ān 7:85

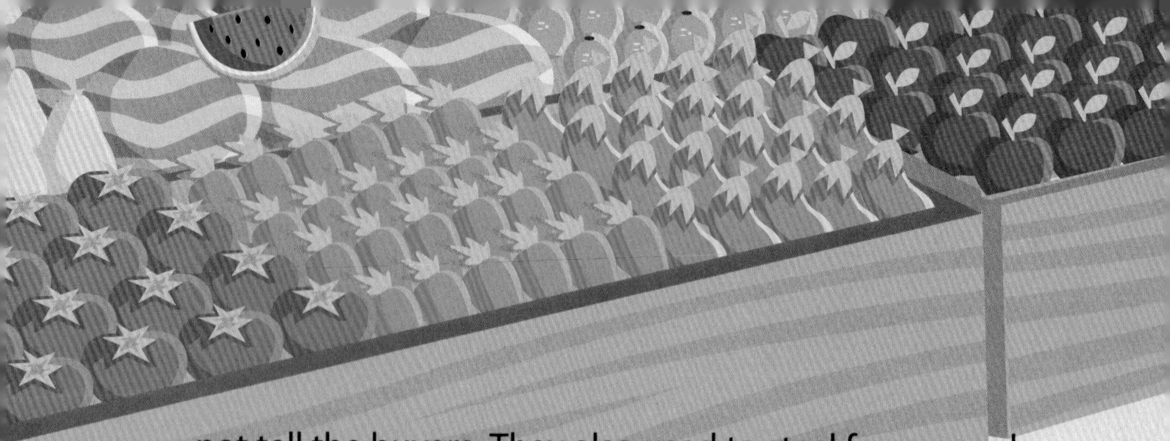

not tell the buyers. They also used to steal from people and attack their caravans. The worst thing they did was not believe in Allāh سبحانه وتعالى alone. Without thinking, they followed the people before them in idol worship.

The people of Madyan turn against Shuʿayb

Living among these people was Shuʿayb عليه السلام. He was from the family of the great Prophet Ibrāhīm عليه السلام. Unlike most of the people around him, he was a very just and truthful person. So he was chosen by Allāh سبحانه وتعالى as a prophet to remind his people to believe in Allāh سبحانه وتعالى alone. He told them to be good, fair and truthful. He promised them that if they worshipped Allāh سبحانه وتعالى alone and were fair in business, Allāh سبحانه وتعالى would give them much more than what they got from cheating and lying.

A few people who were good, believed in Shuʿayb عليه السلام and accepted his message. However, the disbelievers would tease them and tried to stop them from coming to Shuʿayb عليه السلام by bullying them.

Prophet Shuʿayb (عليه السلام) warned them of how Allāh (سبحانه وتعالى) punished others before them, like the people of Nūh (عليه السلام), Hūd (عليه السلام) and Ṣāliḥ (عليه السلام). However, though the people understood Shuʿayb's (عليه السلام) message, they lied to him and threatened him. They said, "We do not understand a lot of what you are saying to us. We see you as a weak person among us and if it wasn't for your family, we would have killed you!" Shuʿayb (عليه السلام) was shocked to hear this and replied, "Do you believe my family is stronger than Allāh?!"

A terrible earthquake

The people's treatment of Shuʿayb (عليه السلام) and his followers got so bad that they told them to either worship their idols or leave Madyan. The disbelievers said to the believers, "You will lose if you follow Shuʿayb!" When Shuʿayb (عليه السلام) continued to call people to Allāh (سبحانه وتعالى), the disbelievers chased him and his followers out of the city.

Shuʿayb (عليه السلام) turned to Allāh (سبحانه وتعالى) and made *duʿāʾ*. It did not take long for the punishment to come. Soon, the

people of Madyan were hit by a powerful earthquake. It left them all dead on the ground. The large amounts of money they had collected did not help them at all. Shuʿayb (عليه السلام) and his followers were saved from the earthquake and were not harmed.

Lessons

- Our wealth is a great test for us.
- We should never be greedy.
- We should be honest when we buy and sell, and never give anyone less than what they deserve.
- Wealth can destroy people if not used properly.

Our wealth is a great test for us.

Daily Ṣalāh: practical

First *rak'ah*

Practical lesson

1. Intention: Stand straight facing the *qiblah* with hands by the sides and make the intention (*niyyah*) to perform a particular prayer in your mind.

2. *Takbīr*: Lift both hands up to the shoulders with palms facing the *qiblah*. The thumbs should be between the earlobes and shoulders for boys and up to the shoulders for girls. Then say, *"Allāhu akbar."*

3. Standing: Then tie your hands with your right hand on top of the left.

- Boys should place their hands just under their belly button.
- Girls should place their hands on their chests.

Then recite *Thanā'*, Sūrah Fātihah, followed by any other *sūrah*.

4. *Rukū'*: Go into *rukū'* by saying, *"Allāhu akbar."* Hold your knees and keep fingers spread out.

- Boys should keep their legs and backs straight.
- Girls should tuck their elbows into their waists and bow just enough so that their hands reach their knees.

Then recite, *"Subḥāna rabbiyal 'aẓīm,"* three times.

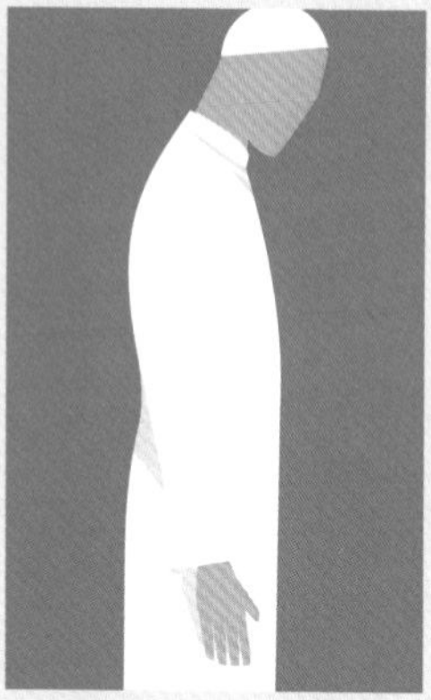

5. Standing after *rukūʿ*: Stand up after *rukūʿ* by saying, "*Samiʿ allāhu li man ḥamidah.*" Make sure your back is straight. Then say, "*Rabbanā lakal ḥamd.*"

6. *Sajdah*: Go into *sajdah* by saying, "*Allāhu akbar.*" Make sure that your knees, hands, nose and forehead are touching the floor. Fingers and toes should be pointing to the *qiblah*.

- Boys should make sure their elbows are not touching the floor and their stomachs are away from their thighs.
- Girls should have their elbows touch the floor and their stomachs should be kept close to their thighs.

Then recite, "*Subḥāna rabbiyal aʿlā,*" three times.

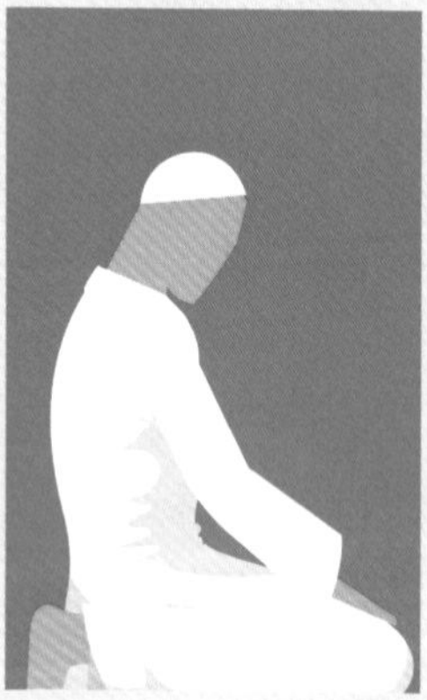

7. Sitting: Then go into the sitting position by saying, "*Allāhu akbar.*" Your palms should be resting on your thighs but not overlapping your kneecaps.

- Boys should sit on the left foot with the right foot up.
- Girls should sit with both feet pointing to the right.

While sitting, recite, "*Rabighfirlī,*" twice.

8. *Sajdah*: Go into *sajdah* again by saying, "*Allāhu akbar.*" Then recite, "*Subḥāna rabbiyal aʿlā,*" three times.

Second *rak'ah*

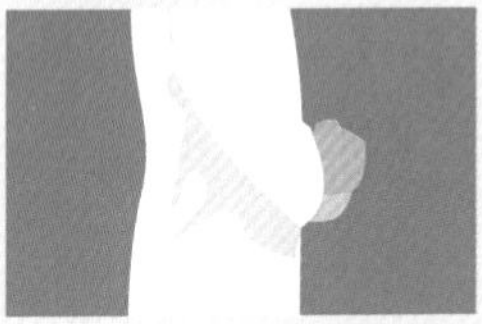

9. Standing: Stand up again by saying, *"Allāhu akbar."* Tie your hands again and recite Sūrah Fātiḥah followed by any other *sūrah*.

10. *Rukū'*: Go into *rukū'* by saying, *"Allāhu akbar."* Then recite, *"Subḥāna rabbiyal 'aẓīm"* three times.

11. Standing after *rukū'*: Stand up after *rukū'* by saying,*"Sami' allāhu li man ḥamidah."* Then say, *"Rabbanā lakal ḥamd."*

12. *Sajdah*: Go into *sajdah* again by saying, *"Allāhu akbar."* Then recite, *"Subḥāna rabbiyal a'lā,"* three times.

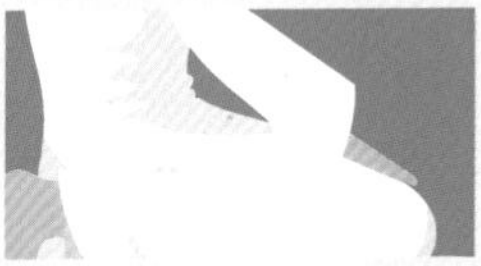

13. Sitting: Come up into a sitting position by saying, *"Allāhu akbar."* Then recite, *"Rabighfirlī,"* twice.

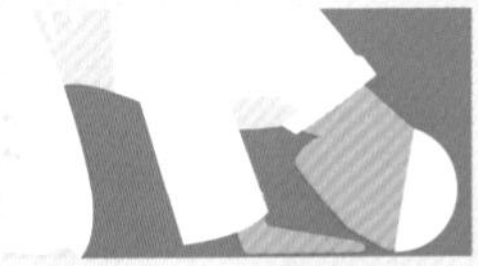

14. *Sajdah*: Go into *sajdah* again by saying, *"Allāhu akbar."* Then recite, *"Subḥāna rabbiyal a'lā,"* three times.

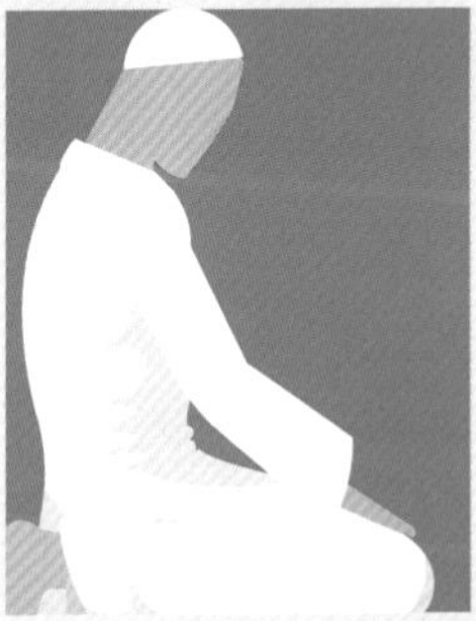

15. Sitting: Come up into a sitting position by saying *"Allāhu akbar."* Recite in full, *"Attaḥiyātu…"*, *"Allāhumma ṣalli…"* and *"Allāhumma innī ẓalamtu…"* Complete your two *rak'ah* prayer by turning your head to your right and saying, *"Assalāmu 'alaikum wa raḥmatullāh,"* and repeat this for the left side straight after.

For a three or four *rak'ah* cycle continue on to step 16 after reciting only *"attaḥiyātu"* in full.

Third *rak'ah*

16. Standing: Stand up again by saying *"Allāhu akbar."* Tie your hands again, and then recite Sūrah Fātiḥah only.

17. *Rukū'*: Go into *rukū'* by saying, *"Allāhu akbar"*. Then recite, *"Subḥāna rabbiyal 'aẓīm,"* three times.

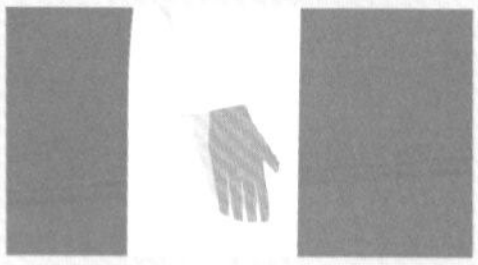

18. Standing after *rukū'*: Stand up after *rukū'* by saying, *"Sami' allāhu li man ḥamidah"*. Then say, *"Rabbanā lakal ḥamd."*

19. *Sajdah*: Go into *sajdah* again by saying, *"Allāhu akbar"*. Then recite, *"Subḥāna rabbiyal a'lā,"* three times.

20. Sitting: Come up into a sitting position by saying, *"Allāhu akbar."* Then recite, *"Rabighfirlī,"* twice.

21. *Sajdah*: Go into *sajdah* again by saying, *"Allāhu akbar"*. Then recite, *"Subḥāna rabbiyal a'lā,"* three times.

For a four *rak'ah* cycle skip step 22 and go to step 23.

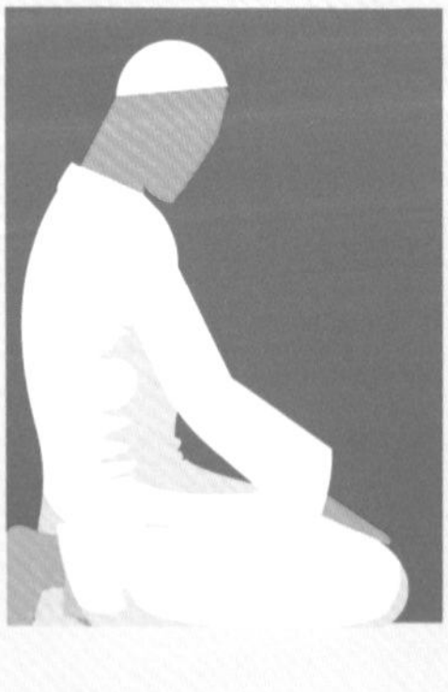

22. Sitting: Come up into a sitting position by saying, *"Allāhu akbar."* Recite in full *"Attaḥiyātu…"*, *"Allāhumma ṣalli…"* and *"Allāhumma innī ẓalamtu…"*

Complete your three *rak'ah* prayer by turning your head to your right and saying, *"Assalāmu 'alaikum wa raḥmatullāh,"* and repeat this for the left side straight after.

Fourth *rak'ah*

23. Standing: Stand up again by saying, *"Allāhu akbar."* Tie your hands again, and then recite Sūrah Fātiḥah only.

24. *Rukū'*: Go into *rukū'* by saying, *"Allāhu akbar."* Then recite, *"Subḥāna rabbiyal 'aẓīm,"* three times.

25. Standing after *rukū'*: Stand up after *rukū'* by saying, *"Sami' allāhu li man ḥamidah."* Then say, *"Rabbanā lakal ḥamd."*

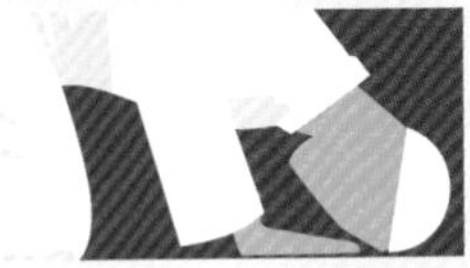

26. *Sajdah*: Go into *sajdah* by saying, *"Allāhu akbar."* Then recite, *"Subḥāna rabbiyal a'lā,"* three times.

27. Sitting: Come up into a sitting position by saying, *"Allāhu akbar."* Then recite, *"Rabighfirlī,"* twice.

28. *Sajdah*: Go into *sajdah* again by saying, *"Allāhu akbar."* Then recite, *"Subḥāna rabbiyal a'lā,"* three times.

29. Final sitting and *salām*: Come up into a sitting position by saying, *"Allāhu akbar."* Recite in full *"Attaḥiyātu…"*, *"Allāhumma ṣalli…"* and *"Allāhumma innī ẓalamtu…"*

Complete your four *rak'ah* prayer by turning your head to your right and saying, *"Assalāmu 'alaikum wa raḥmatullāh,"* and repeat this for the left side straight after.

The open invitation

About three years after the first revelation, Prophet Muḥammad ﷺ started to call people to Islām openly. Before this, he invited people to Islām secretly.

When Allāh سبحانه وتعالى ordered him to give open *daʿwah*, the Prophet ﷺ climbed a mountain called aṣ-Ṣafā and started calling people. In Makkah, this was the quickest way to gather all the people in an emergency.

When people had gathered around the mountain, the Prophet ﷺ first asked them, "If I told you that an army was behind this mountain waiting to attack you right now, would you believe me?" The people replied, "We have never heard you lie." Then he told them that he was a messenger and that he was warning them of a punishment that might strike them if they did not believe in his message.

At first, everyone remained silent. Then the Prophet's uncle, Abū Lahab spoke. He said, "Curse be on you! Is this why you have called us?!"

Some days later, the Prophet ﷺ invited all the great leaders of Makkah to his house for food. After eating, the Prophet صلى الله عليه وسلم again asked who would believe in his message. All the leaders were silent. ʿAli رضي الله عنه, the Prophet's صلى الله عليه وسلم young cousin, stood up and said, "I believe." This made all the guests laugh at him.

The people of Makkah already believed in Allāh سبحانه وتعالى. However, they also believed in other gods. When the Prophet صلى الله عليه وسلم told them that there is only one God, their excuse was that their fathers before them had worshipped these idols. The Prophet صلى الله عليه وسلم explained that their fathers were wrong and that these idols were just stone. But hearing this truth made the people angry. They wanted to hurt him, but his eldest uncle, Abū Ṭālib, would stop them.

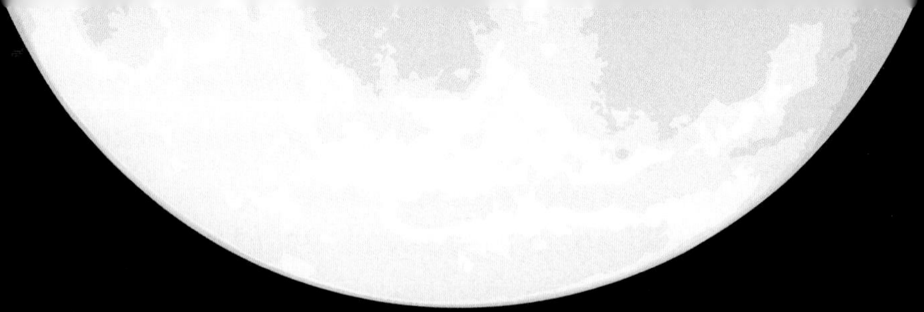

Once, the people came to Abū Ṭālib and complained to him about his nephew, Muḥammad ﷺ. They told him to stop his nephew or they would fight him.

Abū Ṭālib called the Prophet ﷺ and told him what the Quraysh had said. After listening to his uncle, he said, "O my uncle! By Allāh, even if they were to put the sun in my right hand and the moon in my left, I would still not give up this message, until Allāh makes Islām strong or I die for its sake." When Abū Ṭālib heard this he said, "Go, my nephew, and say whatever you like. By Allāh, I will never leave you for anything!"

Daʿwah means to call people to Islām.

Lessons

- Muslims should give *daʿwah* to others.
- We should remain strong when giving *daʿwah*.
- We should put our trust in Allāh سبحانه وتعالى and He will look after us.

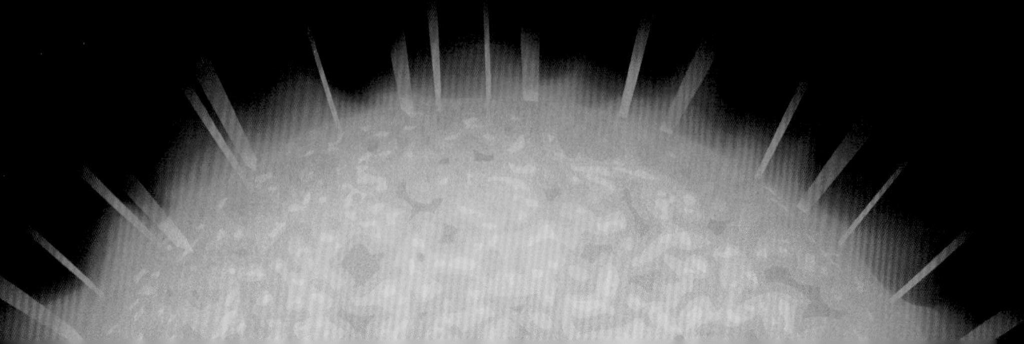

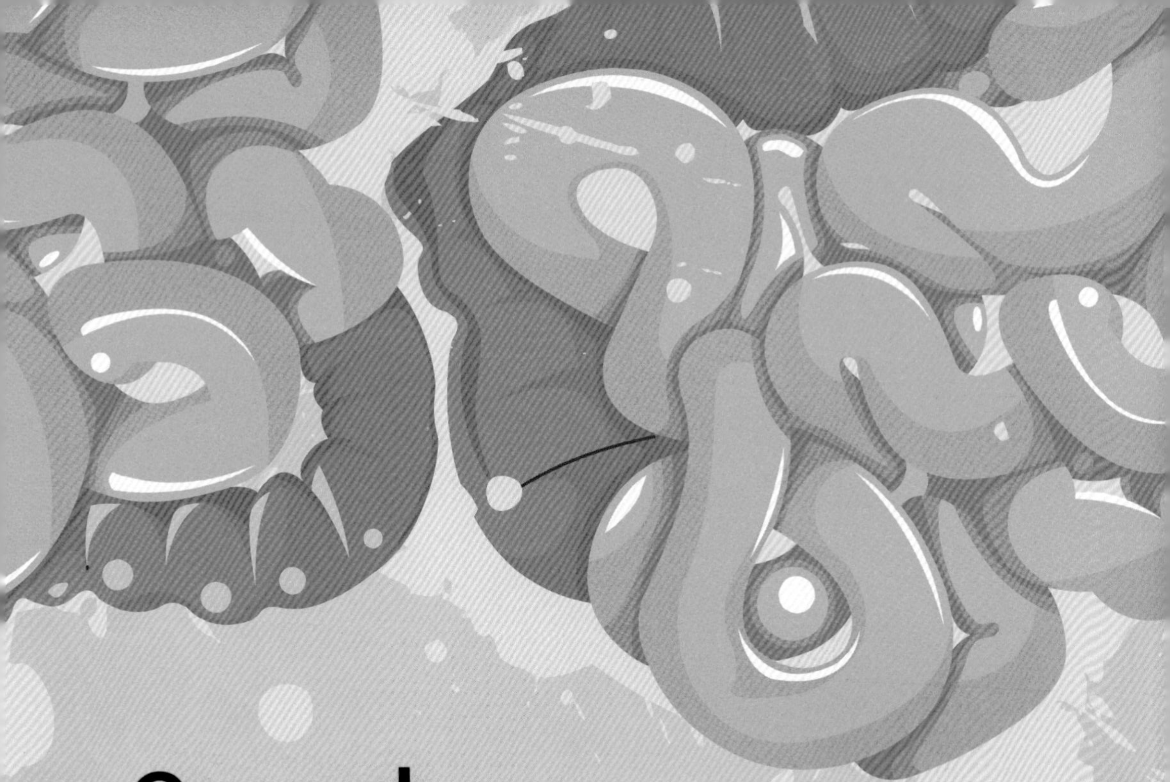

Quraysh abuse the Muslims

As the Prophet ﷺ continued his *da'wah,* it made the Makkans more and more angry. They began to attack and hurt the Muslims.

The sufferings of the Prophet ﷺ

One day, the Prophet ﷺ was doing *sajdah* near the Ka'bah. A man called 'Uqbah ibn Abī Mu'ayṭ came and put the insides of a camel on his back. The Prophet ﷺ could not raise his head. Fāṭimah (رضي الله عنها) rushed to her father and removed it. They were both very upset.

Umm Jamīl was Abū Lahab's wife. She used to throw rubbish at the Prophet's ﷺ door. The Prophet ﷺ would just clean it up and not take revenge.

The story of Musʿab رضي الله عنه

Musʿab ibn ʿUmayr رضي الله عنه was a very handsome young man. He used to wear the best clothes, which most people could not afford. His mother was very rich and made sure that her son lived like a prince. His way of life made him very famous.

When Musʿab رضي الله عنه became a Muslim, his mother became very angry with him. She locked him up in the house. Musʿab رضي الله عنه escaped from his house and came to the Muslims. He left his family, his expensive clothes, and all his money just to be with the Muslims.

Later, when Musʿab رضي الله عنه died, he did not even have enough cloth to cover his entire body. If they covered his head, his feet would be left uncovered and if they covered his feet, his head would be left uncovered. The Prophet ﷺ told his companions to cover his head with a sheet and cover his feet with leaves.

The Story of Bilāl رضي الله عنه

Bilāl رضي الله عنه was an African slave. His master, Umayyah ibn Khalaf used to take Bilāl رضي الله عنه out into the desert at midday, when the sun was at its hottest. Umayyah would make Bilāl رضي الله عنه lie down on the hot, burning sand. Then, he would place a rock on his chest and tell him to leave Islām and worship idols.

But Bilāl رضي الله عنه would reply,
"Aḥad, aḥad."

The word *aḥad* means "one" – "Allāh is one."

One day, Abū Bakr رضي الله عنه, seeing what Umayyah was doing to Bilāl رضي الله عنه, bought Bilāl رضي الله عنه from Umayyah and set him free.

'Ammār رضي الله عنه and his family

- One day, a tribe called Banū Makhzūm took 'Ammār رضي الله عنهما and his mother, Sumayyah رضي الله عنها, and his father, Yāsir رضي الله عنه, outside to be tortured because they were

Muslims. They were left under the blazing sun. The Prophet ﷺ passed by them and saw how they were suffering. He felt very sad. He told them, "Have patience, O family of Yāsir. Your resting place is Paradise." Sumayyah رضي الله عنها was killed by Abū Jahl. She became the first person to die for Islām. Yāsir رضي الله عنه also died because of all the suffering.

> We should always stick to the truth even if people do not like it.

Lessons

- The early Muslims suffered a lot, so that people who came later, could be Muslims. We should make *du'ā'* for them and thank Allāh سبحانه وتعالى for making it easy for us to be Muslims.
- Our Prophet ﷺ was very patient. To be good Muslims, we also need to be patient during difficult times.
- Being kind is sometimes the best way to make an enemy your friend.
- We should always stick to the truth even if people do not like it. Allāh سبحانه وتعالى will always reward us. If nothing else, we will get Paradise.

Breakers of Ṣalāh

It is very important for us to perform our *Ṣalāh* properly and not do anything that will break the *Ṣalāh*. The following things break *Ṣalāh*:

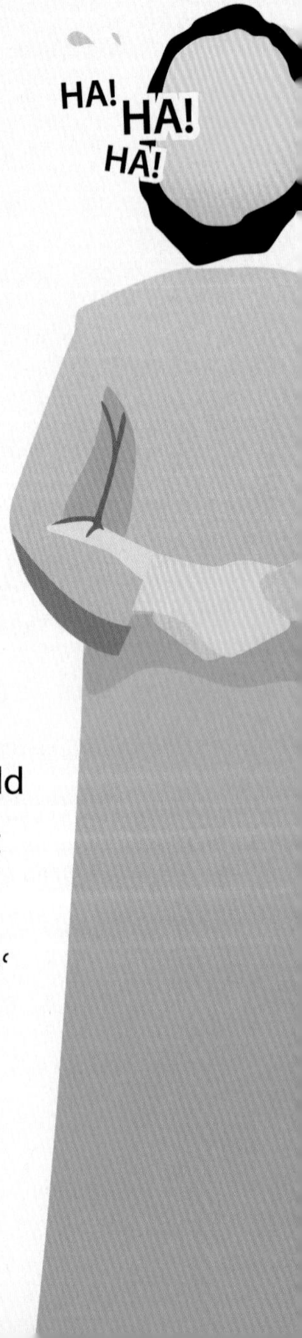

- Things that break *wuḍū'* also break *Ṣalāh*, like vomiting a mouthful.
- To eat or drink, even by accident.
- To talk in *Ṣalāh* - even a little bit - purposely or forgetfully.
- To greet or reply to a person with, *salām* or any other greeting.
- To say, "*Yarḥamukallāh,*" when someone sneezes.
- To laugh loudly, make noise, or say "ah" due to pain or something else.
- *'Amal kathīr*: Doing an action that would make a person watching you think that you are not in *Ṣalāh*.
- To miss out a necessary action like *rukū'* or *sajdah*.
- To turn the chest away from *qiblah*.

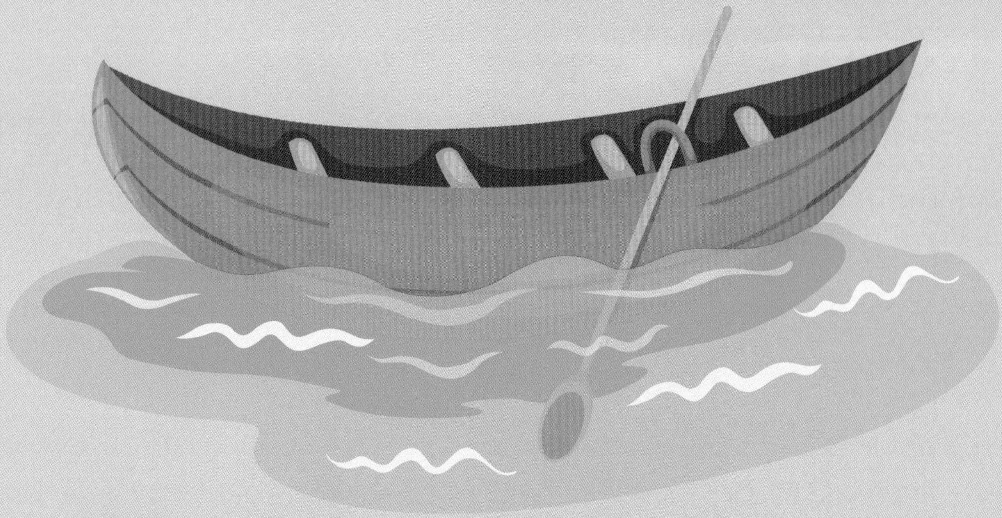

Migration to Abyssinia

Muslims were always being attacked in Makkah. The Quraysh tried their best to harm the Muslims in any way possible. The slaves, the poor and the weak Muslims suffered the most. Many were killed whilst others had to patiently bear the abuse and cruelty they faced at the hands of the Makkans.

There was nowhere the Muslims could go in Arabia to escape the torture and abuse. There was, however, a Christian ruler in Abyssinia, whose title was "Najāshī" (king), who ruled with justice. The Prophet ﷺ recommended a group of Muslims to migrate to Abyssinia so that they could practice their religion freely and openly. This group had 16 people, 12 men and four women. ʿUthmān Ibn ʿAffān رضي الله عنه was also part

of this group along with his wife Ruqayyah (رضي الله عنها), the Prophet's (صلى الله عليه وسلم) daughter.

When the Makkans found out, they tried to chase the group who had left Makkah the night before. However, the Makkans were too late. They became very angry that some Muslims had got away. They now turned their anger towards the Muslims who stayed behind and became even more horrible to them.

Hijrah means to travel from one place to another.

The Prophet (صلى الله عليه وسلم) advised another group of Muslims to migrate (*hijrah)* to Abyssinia, but this time, the group was much larger. Again, they were able to escape the Makkans and made it to Abyssinia, safely. The Makkans were furious and decided to send some men after them to bring them back. The plan was to go to Najāshī and explain that the Muslims had left the religion of their fathers. They would then ask for the Muslims to be returned back to the Makkans, to do with them as they please.

The Makkans sent two of their best men for this job: ʿAmr Ibnul ʿĀṣ and ʿAbdullāh Ibn Abī Rabīʿah, who took expensive gifts with them. They wanted to win the King over so that he would send the Muslims back to Makkah. The two Makkans travelled to Abyssinia and spoke to Najāshī. They said, "Some poor and foolish people amongst us have come to you. Please return them to us". The King replied, "I will not return them until I hear what they have to say."

The King gathered the Muslims in his court and asked them to explain their religion. Jaʿfar Ibn Abī Ṭālib رضي الله عنه gave a speech to the King about Islām and why the Muslims had left the religion of their fathers. He said:

"O King, we were unwise people who worshipped idols. We used to eat dead animals, commit shameful deeds and break family relationships. We used to treat neighbours badly and the strong among us used to be cruel to the weak.

We remained in this state until Allāh sent us a Prophet

who belonged to a very good family among us and whose truthfulness was known to us.

He called us to worship Allāh alone, and to give up the stones and the idols that we and our fathers before us used to worship. He commanded us to speak the truth, to keep our promises and to be kind to our relatives. He ordered us to be helpful to our neighbours, to stop all forbidden acts and to stay away from bloodshed. He told us not to commit shameful acts or steal an orphan's property.

So, our people attacked us and punished us to make us reject our religion. When they became cruel and tried to stop us from practicing our religion, we left for your country. We chose you before anyone else, wanting your protection and hoping to live in justice and peace." Najāshī was very impressed with what the Muslims had to say, and he allowed them to stay in his land.

Negus was very impressed by the Muslims.

The two Makkans made a new plan to make the Muslims look bad. The next day, they went to Najāshī saying that Muslims spoke very badly of Jesus عليه السلام. The King called the Muslims and questioned them about what their religion said about Jesus عليه السلام. Jaʿfar رضى الله عنه recited some verses of the Qurʾān, which described the extraordinary birth of Jesus عليه السلام. Hearing the verses, Najāshī had tears in his eyes; he knew that these were true and noble words. Najāshī said in amazement: "It seems as if these words and those which were revealed to Jesus have come from the same place."

After this, Najāshī told the Muslims that they could stay in Abyssinia for as long as they wished, and they could practice their religion freely. The gifts were returned to the two men, and they were sent back to Makkah; their plan had failed.

TV, music, games and the internet

Allāh سبحانه وتعالى warns us in the Qur'ān that a person's eyes, ears and heart will all be questioned on the Day of Judgement about how they were used to see, hear and learn in this world.[1] For this reason, a Muslim needs to be careful of all the things they see, hear or learn from the television, music, games and the internet.

As good Muslims, we should:

- See, hear or learn things that are useful.
- Not watch or listen to things that are sinful.
- Not waste too much time with entertainment.
- Not allow entertainment or the internet to distract us from our duties to Allāh سبحانه وتعالى.
- Be thankful to our parents who help us to do these things.

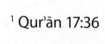

[1] Qur'ān 17:36

TV and online videos

A person can learn many new things through television and online videos. Some programmes teach us useful things, but most are not useful at all. We must stay away from programmes which are sinful. Even when watching useful programmes, a person should be careful not to cross the limits set by Allāh سبحانه وتعالى.

We may also pick up bad habits by watching some programmes. Some people start using bad language or behave in a bad way, copying people and actions they see in TV shows or online. We should, therefore, take care with what we watch on the television or the internet.

Music

All people like to listen to things that are pleasant. The Prophet صلى الله عليه وسلم used to listen to the beautiful readings of the Qur'ān and *nashīds*. *Nashīds* are beautiful songs about Islām that do not have instruments. They can, however, contain the beat of the *daff*.

The purpose of listening to *nashīds* or the Qur'ān is to soften the heart and feel closer to Allāh (سبحانه وتعالى). However, much of the music around us today tends to do the opposite; it makes people forget Allāh (سبحانه وتعالى) or has wrongful content. Some music can even change a person and make them behave badly. This is why 'Abdullāh ibn Mas'ūd (رضي الله عنه) once said, "Music grows hypocrisy in the heart as water grows plants."[2]

Much of the music today, makes people forget Allāh.

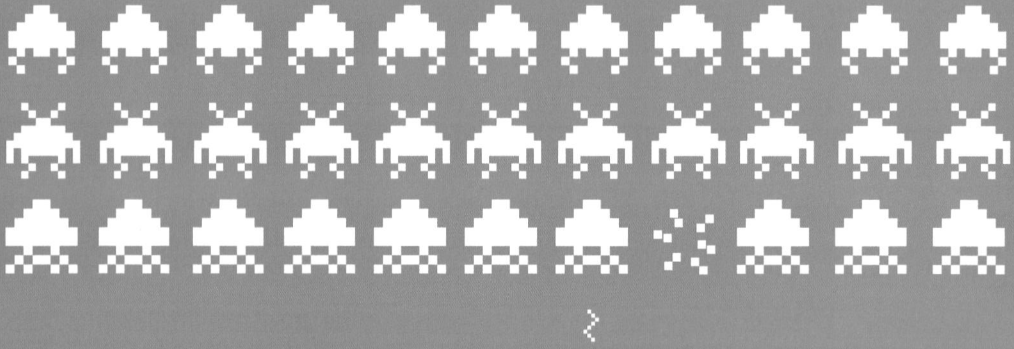

Games

One way of spending our free time is by playing games. Games and playing should not take up all of our free time. They should not distract us from our duties to Allāh (سبحانه وتعالى), our studies or from helping our

[2] Bayhaqī

parents. We should play games that improve our skills and friendship, as well as games that keep us healthy and active.

We should be careful of the types of computer games we play. We need to stay away from computer games that have violence or wrongful things.

If our parents control the time we spend on games or the types of games we play, we should be thankful and not complain. This is because they are helping us get the best in this world and the next. As Muslims, we should try to have a timetable so that we can avoid wasting time or doing useless things.

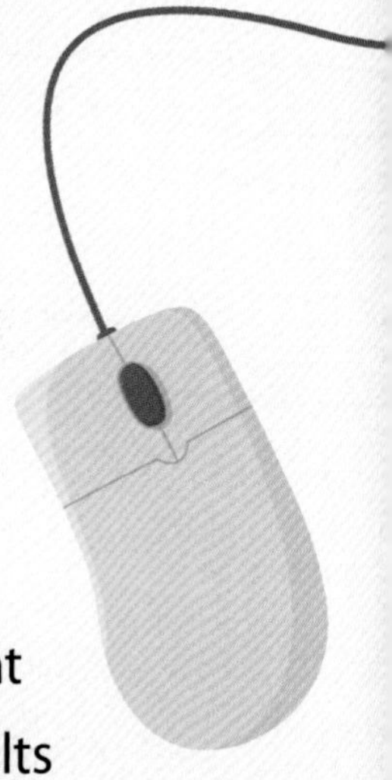

Internet

The internet can be a good tool to use. However, if misused, it can lead to all sorts of trouble. The internet should not distract us from more important and useful activities. We should always first ask adults about the websites we can visit or what type of apps we can use. Also, always ask teachers and parents about what you read and do on the internet. This is because some sites give wrong information or have harmful content. Believing wrong information can spoil our behaviour and beliefs.

Good manners to parents and others

The Prophet صلى الله عليه وسلم said, "Surely I was only sent to perfect the best of manners."[1] For this reason, we need to make sure that we always have good manners. Our good manners should be shown to everyone, including our parents, all Muslims and non-Muslims.

Parents

It is very important for us to make sure that we do not do anything to upset our parents. Allāh سبحانه وتعالى says in the Qur'ān that we should not even say "uff" to our parents for any reason. We should listen to them and do as they say, so long as they do not tell us to do anything wrong.

> "My Lord! Have mercy on them as they had mercy on me when I was young."

We should make sure we do not do anything that will make our parents upset. If our parents become upset with us then Allāh سبحانه وتعالى will be upset with us. For this reason, if we upset our parents we should ask them for forgiveness, straight away.

[1] Ḥākim

We should always try and keep our parents happy because when our parents are happy with us, Allāh سبحانه وتعالى is also happy with us. We should also ask them to make *du'ā'* for us because the *du'ā'* of parents are most definitely accepted by Allāh سبحانه وتعالى.

Respecting everyone

We must respect people at all times, whether in school, at *madrasah* or at home. The following are a few rules we must remember:

Things which we must not do:

We must not hit each other.

- We must not swear at others.
- We must not hit others.
- We must not tease anyone.
- We must not bully anyone.
- We must not steal anything from anyone.
- We must not be rude to others.

Things we must do:

We must be nice to each other.

- We must speak nicely to others.
- We should help others when in need.
- We should always treat others with respect.
- We should talk about good things to one another.
- We should behave with others how we would like them to behave with us.

Abū Hurayrah رضي الله عنه said that once the Prophet صلى الله عليه وسلم asked his Companions, "Who is the one who is bankrupt?" The Companions replied, "The one who has no money and does not own anything is bankrupt." The Prophet صلى الله عليه وسلم then explained that the real bankrupt

person is the one who will come on the Day of Judgement with a lot of good deeds like *Ṣalāh*, fasting and *Zakāh*. However, people whom they swore at, blamed for no reason, stole from or hurt, will come and take their good deeds away in return for the bad things they did to them. If their good deeds run out, they will start giving their bad deeds to that person until, finally, the person will be sent to Hell.[2]

People who are bad to others will be bankrupt on the Day of Judgement.

[2] Muslim

Ḥalāl and ḥarām foods

It is not allowed for a Muslim to eat anything which is *ḥarām*. If a Muslim eats or drinks something that is *ḥarām,* their *du'ā'* may not be accepted. Once the Prophet ﷺ described a man who had travelled a long way, whose hair was untidy and clothes were dusty. He raised his hands to the sky and cried, "My Lord, my Lord!" The Prophet ﷺ then explained, "His food is *ḥarām*, his drink is *ḥarām*, his clothes are *ḥarām* and he has been fed *ḥarām*, so how can his *du'ā'* be accepted?!" The only way for such a Muslim to have their *du'ā'* accepted again is to ask forgiveness from Allāh سبحانه وتعالى.

Things that are *ḥarām* to eat

The following things are *ḥarām* to eat:

- Pig (also called bacon, ham, and pork).
- All animals which hunt for their food (such as lions, wolves, dogs, cats and eagles).
- Dead animals.
- Animals slaughtered without saying the name of Allāh سبحانه وتعالى at the time of slaughtering.
- Gelatine (that comes from the animals mentioned above).
- Alcohol (such as wine, beer, and spirits).

Things that are *ḥalāl* to eat

If any animal besides the above is slaughtered by mentioning the name of Allāh سبحانه وتعالى, it will be *ḥalāl* to eat. The following are some examples:

- Goats
- Sheep
- Cows
- Chickens
- Ducks
- Buffalos
- Camels
- Rabbits

It is also permissible to eat all types of fish.

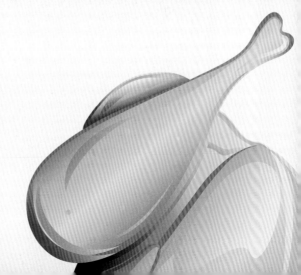

Before we buy anything from the shops, we should check the ingredients and make sure there are no *ḥarām* ingredients, such as:

- Alcohol (such as wine, whisky, rum, and cider).
- Animal fats.
- Non-ḥalāl gelatine (often found in sweets, jellies and deserts).

- Lard (pig fat).
- E471 – an ingredient that is sometimes made from animal fat. If it does not have a vegetarian sign on such a product, do not buy it.

We must also carefully check where we eat. Meat served in some restaurants is *ḥarām*. When eating vegetarian food at restaurants, we need to check the food does not have alcohol and that it has not been mixed with *ḥarām* meat.

Note: Just because you see a "suitable for vegetarians" sign on a product, it does not mean it is *ḥalāl*; the product may have alcohol in it.

010201 400131

The night journey to Jerusalem and the heavens

Isrā' is the journey the Prophet ﷺ made from Makkah to Jerusalem. *Mi'rāj* is the journey he made from Jerusalem to the seven heavens. The whole journey was given to the Prophet ﷺ as a gift from Allāh سبحانه وتعالى, so that he could meet Allāh سبحانه وتعالى.

One night, after Prophet Muḥammad ﷺ prayed *'Ishā'*, Jibrīl عليه السلام came to him with a white animal to take him on the journey of *Isrāʾ*. It was a little larger than a donkey but smaller than a horse, and it was called Burāq. The Burāq is a very fast animal from Paradise.

Jibrīl عليه السلام held the Burāq for the Prophet ﷺ to sit on. They both travelled from Makkah to Jerusalem, where the Prophet ﷺ went to Masjidul Aqṣā. Outside Masjidul Aqṣā there was a ring used by the prophets to tie their animals. The Prophet ﷺ tied the Burāq to this ring. Then the Prophet ﷺ entered the *masjid* where all the prophets from Ādam عليه السلام to ʿĪsā عليه السلام gathered. Prophet Muḥammad ﷺ led them in prayer inside the *masjid*.

After this, the Prophet ﷺ went up to the heavens riding the Burāq. When the Prophet ﷺ and Jibrīl عليه السلام arrived at the first heaven, Jibrīl عليه السلام asked for the gate to be opened. The angel at the gate asked Jibrīl عليه السلام, "Who is with you?" Jibrīl عليه السلام answered, "It is Muḥammad." The angel asked Jibrīl عليه السلام, "Was he sent for? Is it time for him to come to heaven?" Jibrīl عليه السلام replied, "Yes." So, the gate was opened for him and Prophet Muḥammad ﷺ entered the first heaven.

There, Prophet Muḥammad صلى الله عليه وسلم met Prophet Ādam عليه السلام. He then went up to each heaven one after the other. In the second heaven Prophet Muḥammad صلى الله عليه وسلم saw Prophets ʿĪsā عليه السلام and Yaḥyā عليه السلام. They welcomed the Prophet صلى الله عليه وسلم and made *duʿāʾ* for him. The Prophet صلى الله عليه وسلم went to the third heaven, where he met Prophet Yūsuf عليه السلام. Then the Prophet صلى الله عليه وسلم went to the fourth heaven, where he met Prophet Idrīs عليه السلام. In the fifth heaven, the Prophet صلى الله عليه وسلم met Hārūn عليه السلام, the brother of Prophet Mūsā عليه السلام. In the sixth heaven, he met Prophet Mūsā عليه السلام. Each of them welcomed the Prophet صلى الله عليه وسلم and made *duʿāʾ* for him.

Then the Prophet صلى الله عليه وسلم went to the seventh heaven, where he met Prophet Ibrāhīm عليه السلام. Prophet Ibrāhīm عليه السلام is the greatest of the prophets after our Prophet Muḥammad صلى الله عليه وسلم. Then the Prophet صلى الله عليه وسلم went beyond the seven heavens to *Sidratul Muntahā*, an enormous tree with leaves like the ears of elephants.

Thereafter, the Prophet صلى الله عليه وسلم entered Paradise. He saw the different kinds of people that would stay there. He also saw that most of the people of Paradise were people that were poor in this world.

The Prophet ﷺ saw other things on the night journey too. He saw Mālik عليه السلام, the angel in charge of Hellfire. Mālik عليه السلام did not smile at the Prophet ﷺ when they met. When the Prophet ﷺ asked why, Jibrīl عليه السلام answered, "Mālik has not smiled since the day Allāh created him. If he had smiled for anyone, he would have smiled for you."

Then the Prophet ﷺ went further ahead until he reached a place where he heard the sound of pens used by angels who were copying from the Protected Tablet. It is at this place that Prophet Muḥammad ﷺ heard Allāh سبحانه وتعالى.

At first, Allāh سبحانه وتعالى ordered Muslims to offer *Ṣalāh* 50 times a day. When Prophet ﷺ met Mūsā عليه السلام, he told the Prophet ﷺ to ask his Lord to lower the number because Muslims would not be able to cope with so many prayers. So, the Prophet ﷺ asked his Lord to lessen the prayers for his people. Five prayers were taken away. Once again, Mūsā عليه السلام

In this journey we were given the five daily prayers.

told the
Prophet صلى الله عليه وسلم
to ask Allāh سبحانه وتعالى
to lessen the
number of prayers
further. Allāh سبحانه وتعالى
lowered it again, but
Mūsā عليه السلام was still worried
that it would be too much for the followers of the Prophet صلى الله عليه وسلم. In this way, the Prophet صلى الله عليه وسلم kept asking Allāh سبحانه وتعالى to lessen the prayers until it came down to five prayers. Allāh سبحانه وتعالى then said to the Prophet صلى الله عليه وسلم that whoever offers these five prayers, they will get the same reward of praying 50 times a day.

After all these events, the Prophet صلى الله عليه وسلم returned to Makkah. The next day he told everyone what had happened to him the night before. The non-Muslims did not believe him and called him a liar. They made fun of him saying, "it takes us a month to get there, and you are saying you did this in just one night!" They said to Abū Bakr رضي الله عنه, "Look at what your friend is saying. He says he went to Jerusalem and came back, all in one night!" Abū Bakr رضي الله عنه replied, "If that is what he said, it is the truth."[1]

[1] Muslim

Battle of Badr

The Battle of Badr took place in Ramaḍān one and a half years after the *Hijrah*. When Muslims left their homes in Makkah and moved to Madīnah, the Quraysh took all wealth that the Muslims left behind. Abū Sufyān, a leader of the Quraysh, went to Syria with this wealth. There, he sold the wealth and bought weapons and other goods. He planned to use these weapons to attack the Muslims in Madīnah. However, when Prophet Muḥammad ﷺ heard of this plan and that Abū Sufyān was going to pass by Madīnah when returning to Makkah, he came with a small army to capture the weapons and goods.

When Abū Sufyān learnt that the Muslims were on their way to stop him, he quickly changed his route. He also sent a message to Makkah calling for help. When the news reached the Quraysh, they prepared an army with all the weapons, horses and camels they could gather. Altogether, 1,000 people from the Quraysh set out, including 13 of their leaders, to attack the Muslims.

When the Prophet ﷺ found out about the Makkan army coming to attack, he gathered the Muslims and

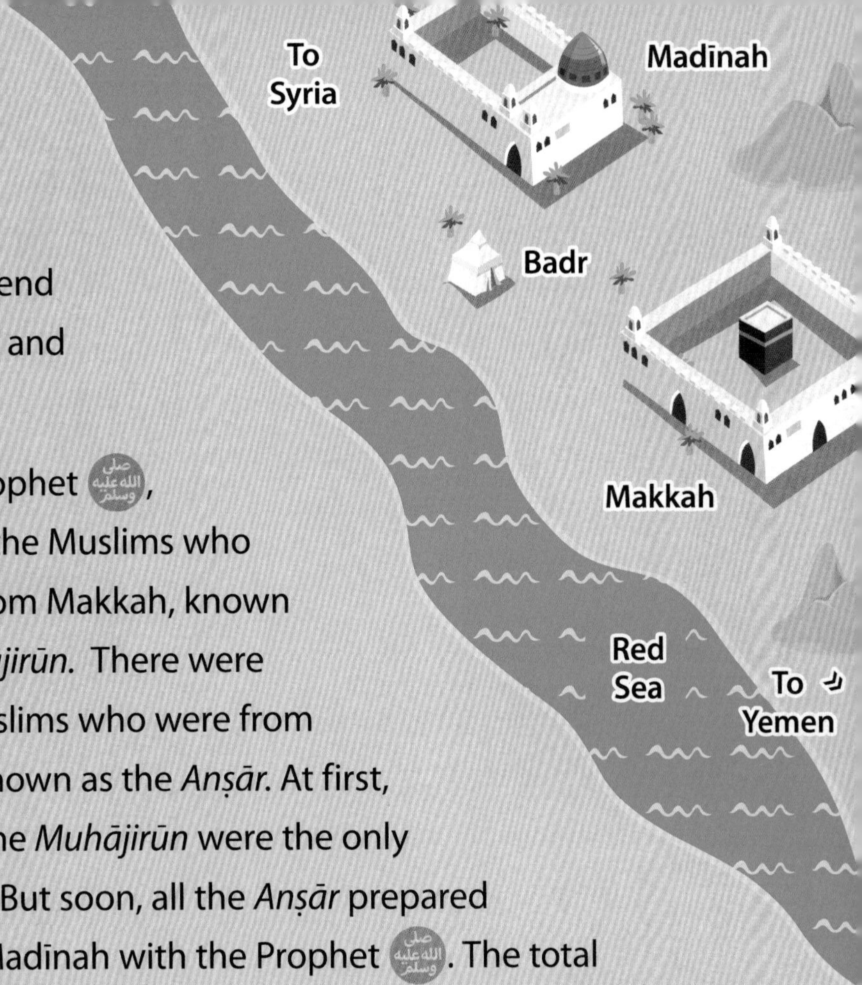

prepared them to defend their homes and families.

With the Prophet ﷺ, there were the Muslims who migrated from Makkah, known as the *Muhājirūn.* There were also the Muslims who were from Madīnah, known as the *Anṣār.* At first, it seemed the *Muhājirūn* were the only ones ready. But soon, all the *Anṣār* prepared to defend Madīnah with the Prophet ﷺ. The total number of Muslims was 313 and they only had two horses and 17 camels between them. Under equipped, they set out to face the mighty army of 1,000 Quraysh.

Before the battle

The Prophet ﷺ left Madīnah with the Muslims and reached water wells at a place called Badr. They arrived there at midnight and made containers to store water from the wells. Then, they waited worried about what was going to happen.

On the night of 17th of Ramaḍān, the Prophet صلى الله عليه وسلم had a shelter made at the top of a hill, so that he could have a good view of the battlefield, and remain in prayer seeking Allāh's help سبحانه وتعالى. When the Quraysh appeared, the Prophet صلى الله عليه وسلم cried to Allāh سبحانه وتعالى, "O Allāh, this is the Quraysh who come with their pride. They have come to fight You and Your Messenger."

In the morning, the Quraysh moved closer, and both the Muslims and the Quraysh took their positions ready for battle. The Prophet صلى الله عليه وسلم arranged the Muslim army and returned to his shelter where he continued to make *du'ā'* to Allāh سبحانه وتعالى asking for help.

One-on-one fights

The Prophet صلى الله عليه وسلم then came out to encourage the Muslims. Three men from the Quraysh stepped forward and challenged three Muslims to a one-on-one fight. The Prophet صلى الله عليه وسلم sent forward 'Ubaydah ibnul Ḥārith, Ḥamzah and 'Alī رضي الله عنهم. They all fought and defeated their opponents; the Muslims could not have asked for a better start.

The battle begins

After the battle began, the Quraysh kept coming to attack the Muslims. Even though they were outnumbered, the Prophet ﷺ kept reminding the Muslims to remain strong and keep their trust in Allāh سبحانه وتعالى. They all fought very bravely and they were not alone; Allāh سبحانه وتعالى sent angels to help them.

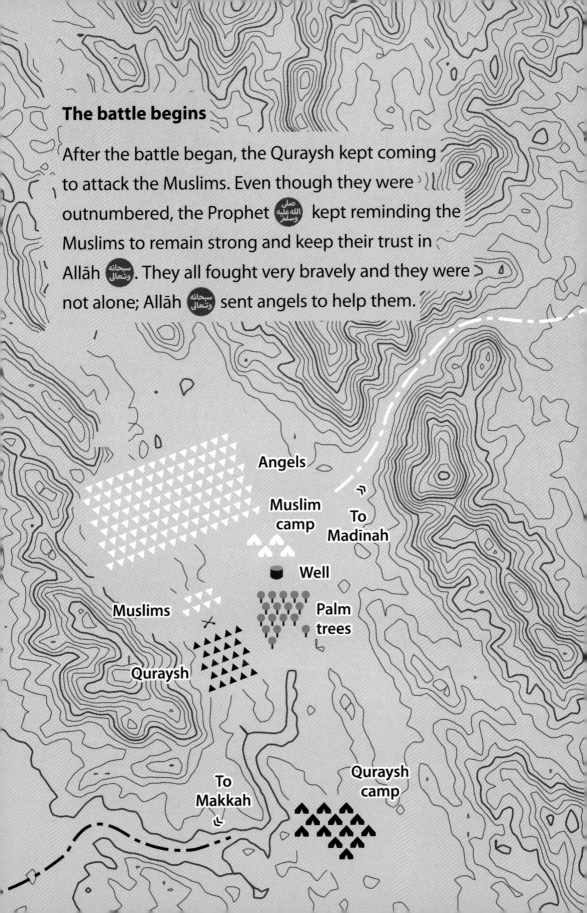

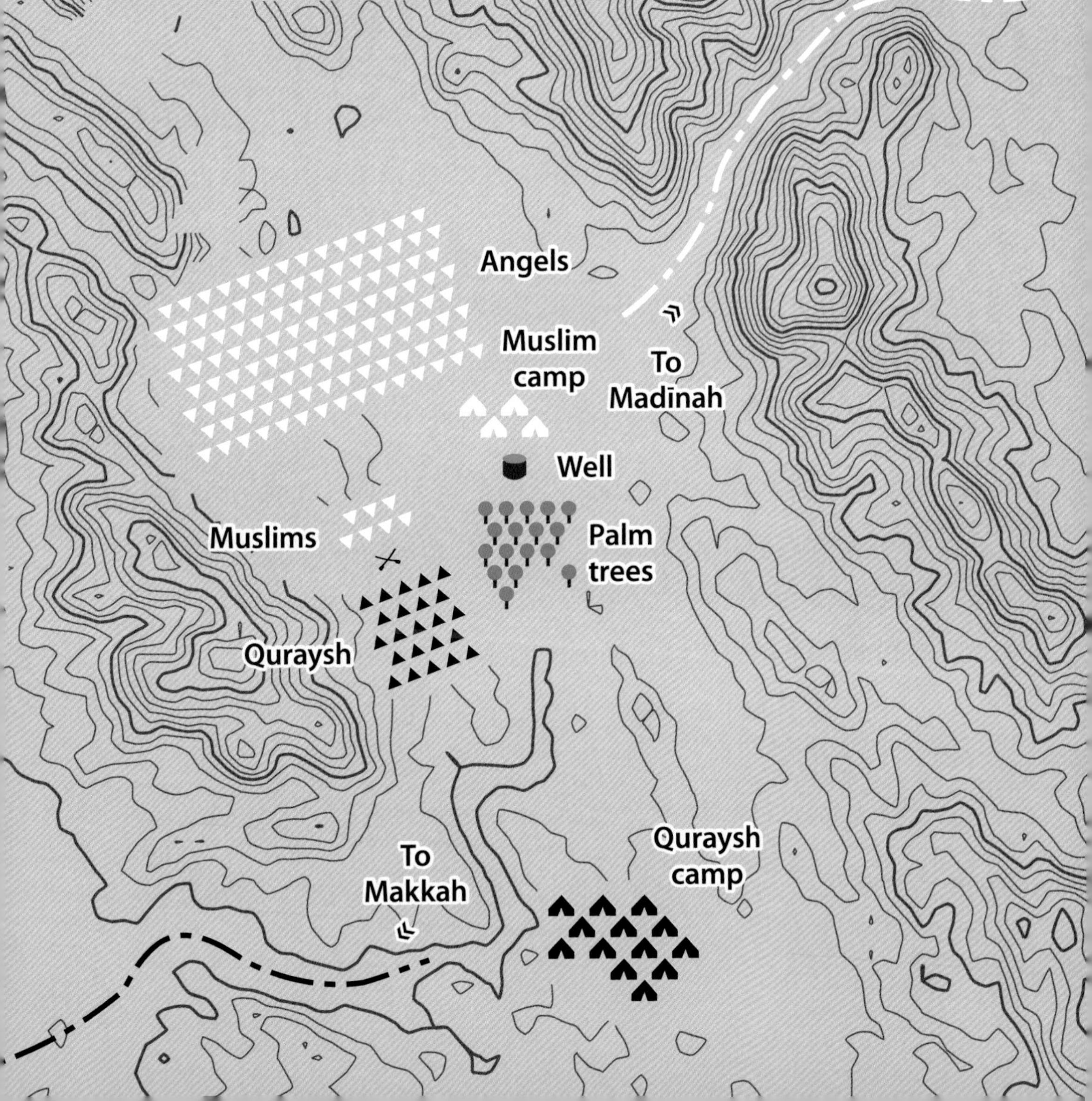

Although the angels were many, they were only seen by a few people. They fought and helped the Muslims in amazing ways. For instance, a companion was chasing an enemy, when all of a sudden, the enemy died as if somebody killed him. Altogether, 5,000 angels came and helped the Muslims.

A clear victory

When victory for the Muslims was certain, the Prophet ﷺ shouted, "Allāh is the greatest!" Allāh سبحانه وتعالى had carried out His promise and granted the Muslims a great victory.

From the Quraysh, 70 people were killed (13 of these were great leaders) and another 70 were captured. From the Muslims, 14 Companions lost their lives.

After years of suffering, Allāh سبحانه وتعالى allowed the Muslims to stand up and defend themselves against the cruel people of Makkah. Now, others living in nearby cities who had hatred for Muslims would think twice before attacking or harming them.

Prisoners of Badr become teachers

The Messenger ﷺ of Allāh سبحانه وتعالى set the prisoners free in return for money and valuables. Those who had nothing, were still given a chance to free themselves; they were freed in return for teaching the children of Madīnah to read and write.

Lessons from Badr

- Muslims strengthen themselves by always trusting Allāh سبحانه وتعالى, no matter what kind of trouble or problems they face.
- It is very important to make *du'ā'* and ask for Allāh's سبحانه وتعالى help during times of hardship and fear.
- Allāh سبحانه وتعالى always fulfils His promise of help and reward to those who obey Him and His Messenger صلى الله عليه وسلم.
- Even though the Quraysh attacked the Muslims, the Prophet صلى الله عليه وسلم asked Muslims to learn from the prisoners, instead of harming them or taking revenge. He was always kind and forgiving, instead of being angry and harsh.

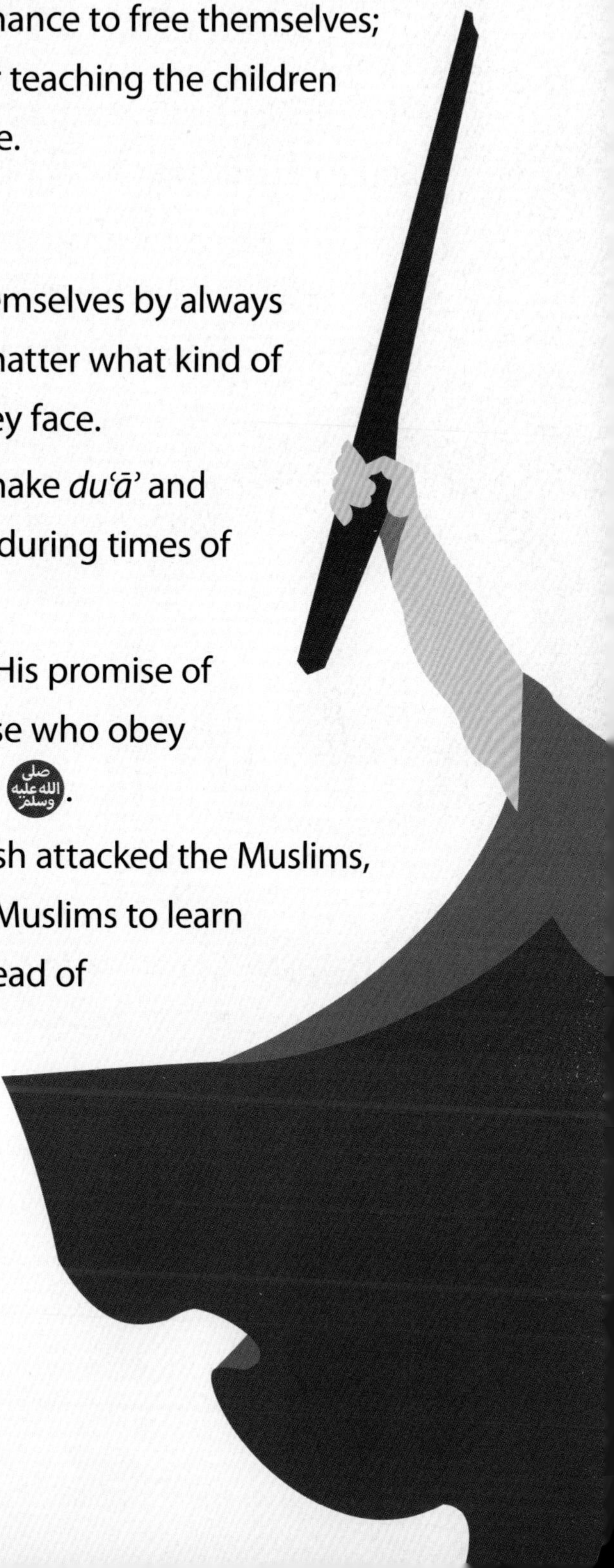

Battle of Uḥud

After the Quraysh were shamefully defeated in the Battle of Badr, they were bitter and angry. They wanted revenge. So, a year after Badr, the Quraysh again gathered a huge army of 3,000 soldiers and set off for Madīnah. The Muslims only had 1,000 men.

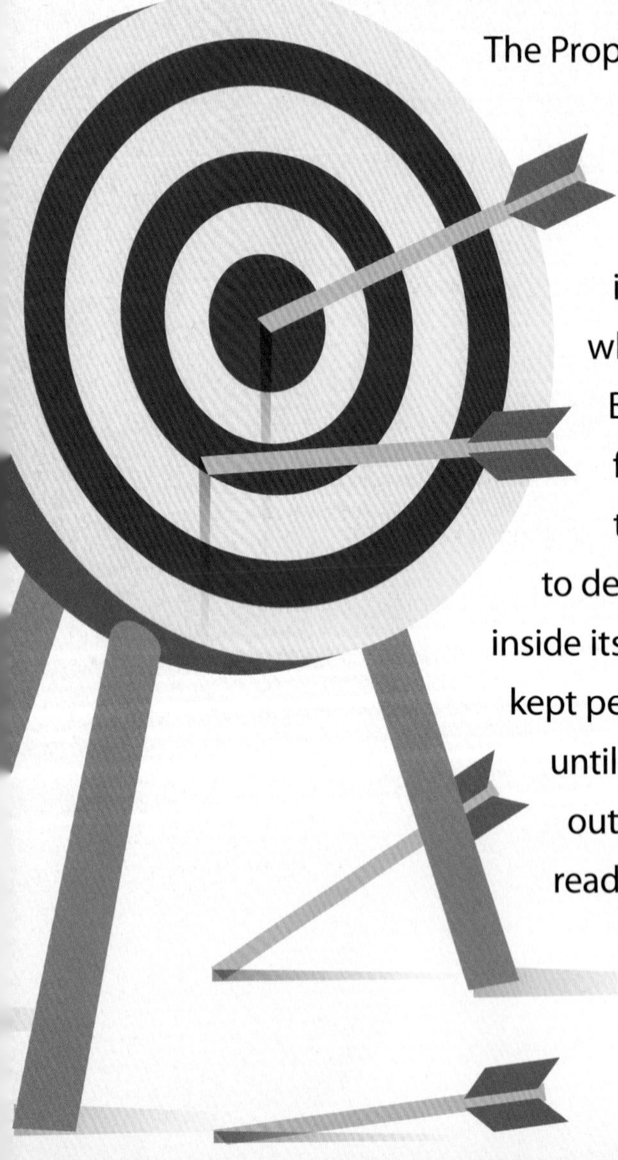

The Prophet ﷺ asked the Muslims if they wanted to go out to fight, or if they wanted to defend Madīnah from inside. Most of the youth who missed the Battle of Badr wanted to go out and fight, while the elders and the Prophet ﷺ wanted to defend Madīnah by staying inside its walls. However, the youth kept persuading the Prophet ﷺ until he finally accepted to go out. He put on his armour, ready for battle. The youth then regretted what they did

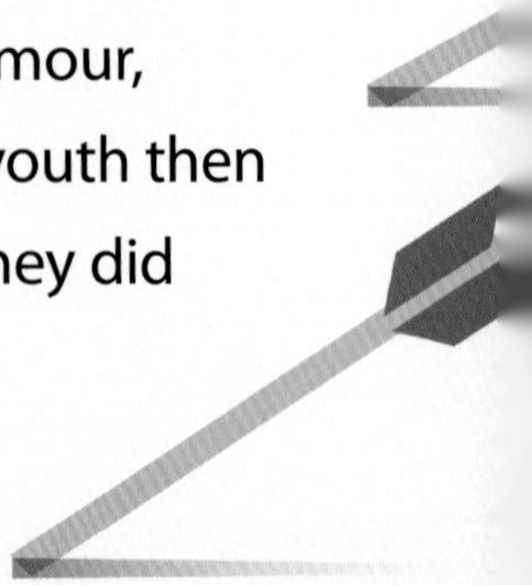

and apologised to the Prophet ﷺ, but it was too late. He said to them, “Once a Prophet puts his armour on to go out and fight, he cannot take it off until he fights.”

As the Muslims set off towards a place called Uḥud, ʿAbdullāh ibn Ubayy, the leader of the hypocrites, shouted out, “The Prophet did not listen to us elders! We are all going to die if we carry on!” Saying this, he turned back with 300 other hypocrites, leaving the Muslims with only 700 men.

On arrival at Uḥud. the Prophet ﷺ spotted a small gap between two mountains. He thought that the Quraysh could use this gap to attack the Muslims, so he placed 50 archers there. He told the archers not to leave from their places at all.

50 archers were placed on a hill and instructed not to leave under any circumstances.

The battle begins

Soon, a fierce battle broke out. The Muslims fought bravery. For example, Abū Dujānah رضى الله عنه who fought with the sword of the Prophet ﷺ, pushed right into the lines of the enemy, fighting very bravely.

Ḥamzah رضي الله عنه, the beloved uncle of the Prophet صلى الله عليه وسلم was known as the "Lion of Allāh." He also fought bravely. No one was able to stop him until Waḥshī, who was not a Muslim yet, attacked him with a spear from behind a rock. The spear pierced Ḥamzah's رضي الله عنه body, and he fell to the ground dying in the way of Allāh سبحانه وتعالى.

Overall, the Muslims were winning the battle. And little later, they started chasing the Quraysh away from Uḥud. As the Quraysh fled, they started to drop their goods so they could get away faster. Some Muslims, thinking that the battle was over, ran to take the wealth that was left behind. Seeing this, some of the archers also started leaving the mountain. The leader of the archers did his best to remind them of the Prophet's صلى الله عليه وسلم order to not leave at all, but it was too late; many had already left, running to take the left behind wealth.

Khālid ibnul Walīd, who was not a Muslim yet, now noticed the open gap between the mountains. So, he came through it with a group of soldiers and killed the remaining archers. He then attacked the Muslims from behind. Seeing this, the fleeing army of Quraysh also turned around and began to fight again. The Muslims were now caught in the middle. During this sudden change, something terrible happened; the Prophet ﷺ fell into a ditch that the enemies had dug. Only a few of his companions were there to protect him. Seeing this, the Quraysh headed straight for the Prophet ﷺ. The few Muslims that were around the Prophet ﷺ defended him, at first with their weapons and then with their bare arms and bodies. One of them, Anas ibn Naḍr رضي الله عنه, was later found with more than 80 wounds on his body.

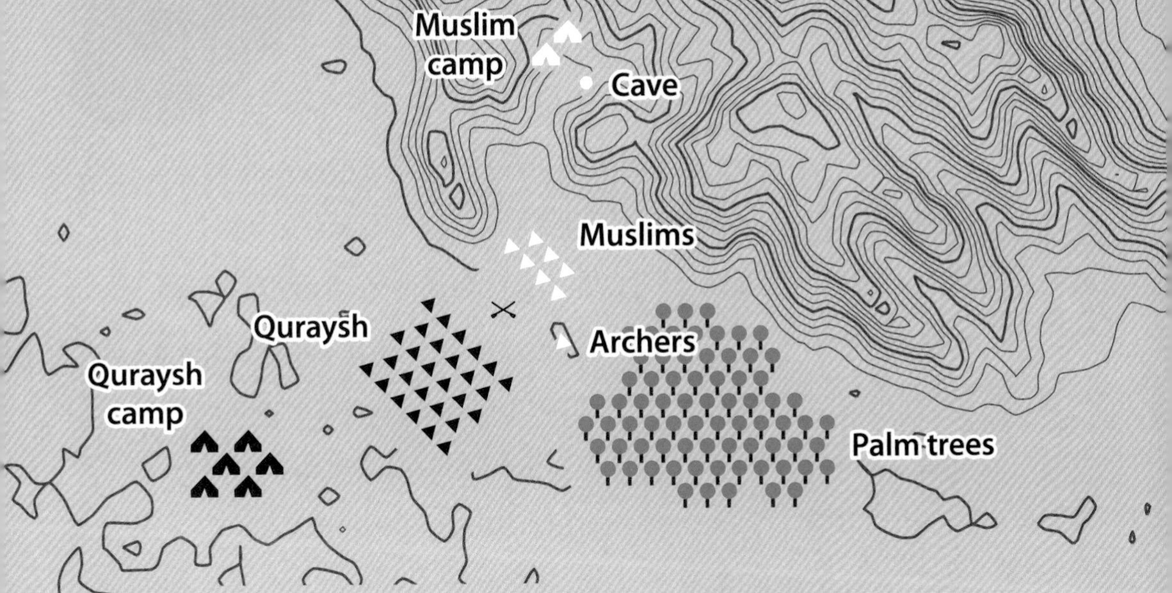

During this chaos, an enemy hit the helmet of the Prophet ﷺ. This broke off two metal spikes which pierced into his cheek, breaking one of his teeth. Abū ʿUbaydah ibnul Jarrāḥ رضي الله عنه pulled the spikes out of the

Prophet's cheeks with his teeth. In doing so, he lost two of his teeth. This sudden change in the battle led to many Muslims being killed.

After the battle

Eventually, more Muslims came to the rescue and together, they went back to a mountain and took shelter. Ubayy ibn Khalaf, one of the leaders of Quraysh, saw them and charged to attack the Prophet ﷺ. When he came close, the Prophet ﷺ took a spear from one of his companions and threw it at Ubayy. It hit him on the neck, making him fall from his horse. Later, Ubayy died before reaching Makkah.

When Abū Sufyān, the leader of the Quraysh, was about to leave, he went to the top of a mountain and shouted, "The luck of war changes. Uḥud is our revenge for Badr!" He then continued to shout, "May the god Hubal rise!" The Prophet ﷺ said, "Get up ʿUmar and tell him that Allāh سبحانه وتعالى is the most High and that we are not the same because our dead are in the Garden of Paradise and your dead are in the Fire!"

After the Quraysh left the battlefield, the Prophet ﷺ and his companions came to search for the Companions who died in the battle. They were very sad with what they saw; the Quraysh had cut the noses and ears of some Muslims. When the Prophet ﷺ saw Ḥamzah رضي الله عنه, he cried so much that he almost fainted. However, neither he nor the Muslims ever did the same to the Quraysh. 70 Muslims were killed, mostly from the Anṣār while 22 of the Quraysh were killed. The Prophet ﷺ gathered the martyrs, prayed over them and then buried them.

Lessons from Uḥud

- When we make decisions with other people, we should not pressure them to accept our view.
- Muslims should never disobey the Messenger ﷺ, as this was a big reason why the battle was lost.
- Muslims love their Prophet ﷺ dearly, more than their own selves.

Keywords/Glossary

A

***Ādāb*:** Good manners and correct behaviour, both inward and outward. Singular: *Adab*.

***Adhān*:** The call to prayer.

***Aḥad*:** One; One of the names of Allāh سبحانه وتعالى.

***'Amal kathīr*:** Excessive actions in prayer which invalidates the prayer.

Al-Amīn: The Truthful One; The Prophet صلى الله عليه وسلم was known as al-Amīn by the Quraysh before prophethood.

***Anṣār*:** The Helpers; Muslims who were the residents of Madīnah and who welcomed the Prophet صلى الله عليه وسلم, believed in him and assisted him.

***'Aṣr*:** The mid-afternoon prayer; One of the five daily prayers.

***At-taḥiyyātu*:** The *du'ā'* recited during the sitting position of *Ṣalāh*, known as *tashahhud*.

B

Badr: A place near the coast, about 95 miles south of Madīnah where, in 2 AH, the Battle of Badr took place.

***Bismillāh*:** In the name of Allāh; A phrase used by Muslims before they do any action.

Book of Deeds: A book in which all the good and bad actions of an individual are recorded.

Black Stone: *Al-Ḥajar al-Aswad*; the black stone located in one of the corners of the Ka'bah.

D

***Da'wah*:** Calling and inviting people to worship Allāh سبحانه وتعالى by following the Messenger of Allāh صلى الله عليه وسلم.

Day of Judgment: A day in the Hereafter where Allāh سبحانه وتعالى will gather all of humankind and jinn.

***Du'ā'*:** Praying, supplicating and asking Allāh سبحانه وتعالى to fulfil our needs and for His blessings.

F

***Fajr*:** One of the five daily prayers performed after dawn and before sunrise.

G

Gelatine: A colourless or slightly yellow, transparent, protein formed by boiling the specially prepared skin, bones, and connective tissue of animals and used in foods, drugs, and photographic film.

H

Ḥadīth: The sayings, actions and approvals of our beloved Prophet صلى الله عليه وسلم.

Ḥaḍramawt: A historic city in Yemen.

***Ḥalāl*:** Lawful: all things lawful and permissible in Islām.

***Ḥarām*:** Unlawful; Anything that Allāh سبحانه وتعالى or His Messenger صلى الله عليه وسلم have prohibited.

***Hijrah*:** Migration; The journey of the Prophet صلى الله عليه وسلم and the Muslims when they left Makkah to settle in Madīnah.

Hubal: One of the chief idols worshiped by the Quraysh before Islām.

I

Idol: An image or statue used as an object of worship.

***Imām*:** The one who leads prayers in the *masjid*.

Iram: The city of Ād, also known as, the city of a thousand pillars. Its exact location still remains uncertain although historians have speculated it to be in Oman due to the remains excavated there.

'Ishā': The night prayer; One of the five daily prayers.

Al-Isrā wal Mi'rāj: The night journey undertaken by the Prophet ﷺ to Jerusalem and the heavens.

J

Jerusalem: The capital of Palestine and the third holiest city in Islām.

K

Ka'bah: The House of Allāh ﷻ in Makkah.

M

Madīnah: The city of the Prophet ﷺ previously known as Yathrib.

Maghrib: The sunset prayer; One of the five daily prayers.

Makkah: The city in which the Prophet ﷺ was born and the Qur'ān was revealed.

Martyr: A person who suffers death for the Truth.

Masjid: A house of Allāh ﷻ where Muslims pray. Also known as a mosque.

Masjidul Aqṣā: The great *masjid* of Jerusalem.

Mu'adhdhin: One who makes the call to prayer. See *adhān*.

Muhājirūn: The Migrants; The Muslims who migrated (did *Hijrah*) from Makkah to Madīnah.

N

Nashīd: Islamic song or poem.

Negus: Used formerly as a title for emperors of Ethiopia.

P

Prophet: A pious male chosen and sent by Allāh ﷻ to a nation or community to guide the people and spread Allāh's ﷻ words and guidance on earth. When used as "the Prophet" it refers to the Prophet Muḥammad ﷺ.

Q

***Qiblah*:** The direction faced in prayer which is towards the Ka'bah in Makkah.

Quraysh: One of the most powerful tribes of Arabia. The Prophet Muḥammad ﷺ was from this tribe. The tribe had great influence and power, both spiritually and financially before and after Islām.

S

Aṣ-Ṣafā: A small mountain in Makkah now located in al-Masjid al-Ḥarām.

***Ṣaḥābī*:** A Companion of the Prophet ﷺ, who saw the Prophet ﷺ in the state of Islām and then died on that same Islām.

Ṣalāh: The prayer, particularly the five daily prayers.

***Salām*:** To say, *"As-salām 'alaykum wa raḥmatullāh,"* at the end of the prayer. This phrase is also used as a greeting.

Scroll: An ancient book in the form of a roll of parchment.

Shirk: To make partners with Allāh سبحانه وتعالى by worshipping something other than Him; like trees, stones, idols and stars.

T

***Ṭahārah*:** A general term for purification and purity.

***Taḥiyyatul Masjid*:** Two *rak'ahs* which are prayed on entering the *masjid*.

U

Uḥud: A mountain just outside of Madīnah, where in 3 AH the Muslims lost a battle against the idol worshippers of Makkah.

V

Virtues: The rewards of actions.

Z

Zabūr: Psalms: the revelation sent to Dāwūd عليه السلام.

***Zakāh*:** Charity that Muslims must give to the needy from part of their wealth. *Zakāh* is a pillar of Islām.

***Ẓuhr*:** The afternoon prayer; One of the five daily prayers.

Syllabus overview
Safar Learn about Islam Series

Book 1

Aqīdah

Who am I?
Paradise and Hell
Shahādah
The six articles of faith
The four angels and their jobs
Belief in Allāh
Belief in His angels
Belief in His books
Belief in His messengers
Belief in the Day of Judgement
All good and bad is from Allāh

Fiqh

The five pillars of Islām
Keeping clean
Using the toilet
How to do *wuḍū'*
Names of the five daily *Ṣalāh*
Times of the five daily *Ṣalāh*
Basic *Ṣalāh* positions
Fasting (*Ṣawm*)
Zakah and *ṣadaqah*
Ḥaj
Islamic months

History

Story of *Nabī* Ādam
Story of *Nabī* Nūḥ
Story of *Nabī* Ibrāhīm
Story of *Nabī* Yūnus
Story of *Nabī* Mūsā
Story of *Nabī* ʿĪsā

Sīrah

Story of *Nabī* Muḥammad

Personal/Language development

Saying *salām*
Alif to *yā* of little reminders
Classroom rules
Everyday *du'ā's*
Arabic alphabet

Book 2

Aqīdah

Names of Allāh
Jannah and Jahannam
Six articles of faith
Jibrīl teaches us religion

Fiqh

Five pillars of Islām
Basic cleanliness
When and how to perform *wuḍū'*
Actions that break *wuḍū'*
How to perform *ghusl*
Prayer times
Ṣalāh: two *rak'ahs*
Ṣalāh: three *rak'ahs*
Ṣalāh: four *rak'ahs*

History

Before Prophet Ādam
Ādam's Creation
Ādam on Earth
Prophet Nūḥ
The boy and the king

Sīrah

Abdul Muṭṭalib
Year of the elephant
The Story of Ḥalīmah
Journey to Syria
Rebuilding the Ka'bah
Beginning of revelation
'Umar accepts Islām
The boycott
Hijrah
Life in Madīnah

Personal development

Bismillah
Adab in the classroom
Manners and friends
Deeds

Book 3

Aqīdah

Names of Allāh
Paradise and Hell
Angels
Books from Allāh
Prophets of Allāh
Life after death

Fiqh

Cleanliness
Manners of using the toilet
Revision of *rak'ahs*
Daily *Ṣalāh*: theoretical
Daily *Ṣalāh*: practical
Breakers of *Ṣalāh*
Ḥalāl and *ḥarām* foods

History

The story of Hābīl and Qābīl
Prophet Hud and the people of 'Ād
The companions in the cave
Prophet Ṣālih and the people of Thamūd
Prophet Shu'ayb and the people of Madyan

Sīrah

The open invitation
Quraysh abuse the Muslims
Migration to Abyssinia
The night journey to Jerusalem and the heavens
Battle of Badr
Battle of Uḥud

Personal development

Respecting people
Manners of eating and drinking
Manners of the *masjid*
Good manners to parents and others
TV, music, games and internet
Why Muslims perform *Ṣalāh*

Book 4

Aqīdah

Names of Allāh ♡
Angels and their duties
Gardens of Paradise and fire of Hell
Signs of the Last Day
Day of Judgement
Miracles
Characteristics and duties of the prophets
Sins and *shirk* ♡ 📕
Love for the Prophet ♡ 📕

Fiqh

Najāsah
Model *wuḍū'* 🏃 ♡
Model *ghusl* 🏃
Model *tayammum* 🏃
Model *Ṣalāh* 🏃 ♡ 📕
Islamic calendar
Fasting and Ramaḍān ♡ 📕

History

Prophet Ibrāhīm ♡ 📕
Story of Dhul Qarnayn

Sīrah

Companions of the Prophet
Battle of the Trench
Ḥudaybiyyah

Personal development

Virtues of actions
Importance of *Ṣalāh*
Good character and brotherhood ♡

Book 5

Aqīdah

Names of Allāh ♡
Angels, books and messengers
From Hell to Paradise
Signs of the Last Day
Description of the Last Day
Death

Fiqh

Types of rulings
Wuḍū': *farḍ*, *sunnah* and *makrūh* ♡
Ghusl: *farḍ*, *sunnah* and *makrūh* ♡
Times of *Ṣalāh*
Forbidden and disliked prayer times
Basics of *tayammum* 🏃
Sunnah mua'kkadah and *ghayr mua'kkadah*
Witr 🏃 ♡
Farḍ acts of *Ṣalāh* 🏃 ♡
Breakers of *Ṣalāh*
Disliked acts in *Ṣalāh*
Rules and rewards of fasting ♡ 📕

History

Prophet Ayyūb
Prophet Yūnus ♡
Dāwūd and Jālūt
Prophet Dāwūd

Sīrah

Letter to Heraclius
Conquest of Makkah

Personal development

Making *Ṣalāh* part of life
Islamic dress code 🏃
Good character and sins ♡ 📕

Book 6

Aqīdah

Who is Allāh and why did He create us?
Tawḥīd and *shirk* ♡ 📕
Seeing Allāh in Jannah
Character of the Prophet

Fiqh

Rulings of *wuḍū'*
Rulings of *ghusl*
Adhān and *Iqāmah* 🏃 ♡
Ṣalāh drill 🏃 ♡
Adā and *qaḍā*
Sajdah sahw 🏃
Ṣalāh in congregation and *sutrah* 🏃
Translation of *Ṣalāh* ♡ 📕
Personal hygiene and maturity
Rulings of fasting ♡ 📕
Ḥalāl and *ḥarām* consumption ♡
Model *janāzah Ṣalāh* 🏃 ♡ 📕

History

Prophet Sulaymān
Prophet Isḥāq and Ya'qūb

Sīrah

Ḥunayn and Ṭā'if
Last days of the Prophet

Personal development

Obedience to Allāh and His Messenger
Virtues of the Qur'ān ♡ 📕
Ṣalāh: our link with Allāh
Concentration in *Ṣalāh* 🏃 ♡ 📕

🏃 Practical lesson; ♡ Overlap with the Learn by Heart Series; 📕 Overlap with the Learn Arabic Series

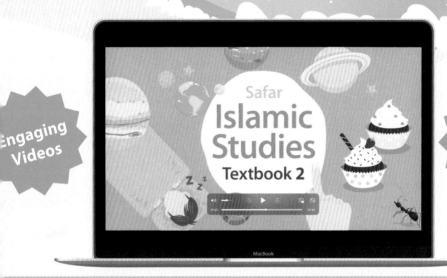

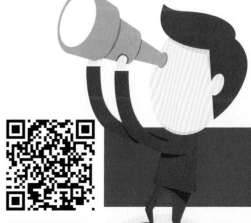